THE RULE *of* FAITH

THE
RULE OF
FAITH

SCRIPTURE, CANON, AND CREED IN A CRITICAL AGE

edited by Ephraim Radner
and George Sumner

MOREHOUSE PUBLISHING
HARRISBURG, PENNSYLVANIA

Morehouse Publishing
P.O. Box 1321
Harrisburg, PA 17105

Morehouse Publishing is a division of the Morehouse Group.

"In Accordance with the Scriptures: Creed, Scripture, and 'Historical Jesus'" reprinted from *Word Without End: The Old Testament as Abiding Theological Witness* (Grand Rapids: Eerdmans, 1998). Used by permission.

Cover art: Giraudon/Art Resource, NY. Metropolitos, John. *Christ as Redeemer and Source of Life.*

Cover design by Rick Snizik

Library of Congress Cataloging-in-Publication Data

The rule of faith : Scripture, canon, and creed in a critical age /
   edited by Ephraim Radner and George Sumner.
      p.   cm.
   Rev. lectures presented at a conference held in Jan. 1997 in
Charleston S.C., sponsored by Scholarly Engagement with Anglican
Doctrine.
   Includes bibliographical references.
   ISBN 0-8192-1741-7 (pbk.)
   1. Jesus Christ—Person and offices—Doctrines—Congresses.
2. Episcopal Church—Doctrines—Congresses.   3. Jesus Christ—Person
and offices—Biblical teaching—Congresses.   4. Bible—Evidences,
authority, etc.—Congresses.   I. Radner, Ephraim, 1956-   .
II. Sumner, George R., 1955-   .   III. Scholarly Engagement with
Anglican Doctrine (Society)
BT202.R75   1998
232.9'03—dc21   98-28271
                                                                       CIP

Printed in the United States of America

CONTENTS

Introduction

The Rev. Dr. George R. Sumner and The Rev. Dr. Ephraim Radner

T*he Rule of Faith* is composed of revised lectures that were presented at a conference held in Charleston, South Carolina, in January 1997. This conference was sponsored by Scholarly Engagement with Anglican Doctrine (SEAD), an independent society committed to encouraging theological discussion in the Episcopal Church.

The theme of the conference was "Who is Jesus? The Christ of Creed and Covenant." A prominent voice in constructive biblical theology, Professor Brevard Childs, and several younger theologians working in the Episcopal Church sought to bring into conversation this matter of popular concern. To some extent this question was already being discussed; a few of the presenters either had studied under Professor Childs or, as colleagues, had engaged with him in such common discussions and projects. In the shadow of increasingly well-publicized debate over the historical basis for traditional claims about Jesus (cf. the high-profile work of the Jesus Seminar), the conference was designed to be an opportunity for critical reflection on the rejection of these orthodox assertions. Several hundred people of the Church gathered to hear Professor Childs examine the character of the Bible as Christian Scripture, and to see that character put to work in the enunciation of traditional affirmations about Jesus given in the Nicene Creed, through the accompanying presentations.

It would be wrong, however, to judge these essays as a collection of conservative defenses of ancient and precritical dogma against the discomfitting forays of contemporary historical criticism. Any perceptive reader will immediately see how varied are the intellectual perspectives, religious styles, and even doctrinal interests of the contributors. In fact, this is so much the case that one could wonder about the thread that holds these perspectives together. The first thing to emphasize, then, is that these essays do not aim to present a systematic doctrine, wherever the location on the theological spectrum. Even less so do these essays attempt to attack "dangerous" critical activities on the part of academic theological subversives. Rather, they offer a simple display of what it might mean to think scripturally about Jesus in the context of the Christian Church as it indwells a critical (or possibly uncritical) culture like our own.

Professor Childs, in an admirable summary, and at times even a novel elaboration, of some of his most ground-breaking studies on the character and reference of the Scriptures, straightforwardly uncovers, through juxtaposition, the inadequacy of many contemporary questions about the nature of the Bible and the Jesus it describes. Woven around his remarks, in the form of reflection by other authors on articles of the creed, are first-order examples of how questions that take seriously the intrinsic nature of Scripture might well be asked. They are neither uncritical nor ahistorical questions; they are merely questions that are appropriate to the subject matter described and embodied by Scripture.

This collection of essays, then, is not designed to present a set of self-proclaimed intellectual norms—ranged polemically against a popular enemy—about how to understand Scripture and Jesus in relation to each other. It is intended, rather, to demonstrate a reflective practice in the face of that relation. Readers who themselves delve into this practice, however cautiously and critically, will honor the volume's purpose.

Practices, however, can be described and analyzed according to an ordered logic of their own. If historical-criticism, as it has deconstructed the scriptural Jesus, has erred by pressing the wrong questions on a text such as the Bible, then surely there is some articulate way of describing an alternate means to honestly apprehend the Scriptures' speech. One way to get at such a description is to state openly an aspect of the Christian commitments held by those who attended the Charleston conference. What brought these scholars, pastors, and laypeople together? Something, we believe, that they hold in common with many other Christians of our era, if in a somewhat more self-conscious, perhaps even more beleaguered, way than in times past. Their common focus, given through the orienting lens of the conference's sponsoring organization, was a shared desire to reclaim and inhabit afresh the theological center of the Christian faith, even as they perceived around them a forgetfulness of the faith, now too often ideologically charged and polarized.

This leads us to the second feature of these essays, one we will discuss in detail. "Retrievalist" groups like SEAD, who are looking for the "center," tend to work under banners like "dynamic" or "generous orthodoxy," which attempt to qualify some suspect conservative commitment with a more liberal spice. Or they have tried to hold together two culturally contradictory stances, like "evangelical" and "catholic." However, beyond such broad orientations of paradox, which strive to congeal centrifugal religious forces, there are particular issues at stake in this kind of attitude that have concrete implications for the practice of the Christian faith. And in our time—perhaps in most times—the real theological struggle remains one over the Scriptures: their authority, vital content, and formative interpretation. This was in large part the reason for a conference that brought together a biblical scholar with theological concerns and theologians with reflections on Scripture's authority.

In what, though, does the theological center consist when it comes to Scripture? The current debate within our churches regarding the matter of sexuality has uncovered such an antagonized confusion over the specifically scriptural question that the yearning for such a center has been, ironically, fueled with a renewed though thoroughly uncritical energy. The easier route, in this context, is to define such a center negatively by distinguishing it from fundamentalism on the one hand and from unshriven historical criticism on the other. The eschewal of a positive content for the scriptural center that such a definition entails may, of course, be appealing in the present ecclesial landscape. But the simple self-definition of the orthodox center simply as the mean between opposing extremes will not suffice.

For Anglicans, at any rate, the affirmation of such a mean is hardly a new move, reclothing in modern garb a self-understanding that dates to the early seventeenth century and that has presided over the intellectual evisceration of the denomination's religious character for some time now. Twenty years ago Bishop Stephen Sykes, in his *Integrity of Anglicanism*, showed with ruthless clarity how such a move brought Anglicanism to the vacuous defense of ambiguity for its own sake, and relieved its theologians from the work of showing how contraries actually did converge in a higher truth. Such a promised convergence, we must note, is a starkly critical challenge.

The governing image one adopts in describing the relative character of orthodoxy is therefore obviously important. The spatially horizontal figure of the "mean"—given in the famous *via media* ("middle way") conceit attributed to Anglican sensibilities—has done much to restrict theological discourse particularly as it is tied to Scripture. After all, how does scriptural truth act in a place between extremes? Is the middle way logically related to the "narrow way" of Jesus? Is it possible to see the gospel as a compromise between convictions? Is the cross something that balances opposing weights? Is divine judgment or divine grace ever found and offered in a center that meets its object only halfway? Simply raising such questions about a theological mean displays the image's distance from the meat of scriptural language.

To speak of the theological mean that interpretively approaches the Bible is to demand a mangling of scriptural terms whose intensity and uninhibited grasp altogether work on another plane. A once standard work on the mean, Timothy Puller's seventeenth-century treatise on "The Moderation of the Church of England," sought to establish a reasonable balance between Protestant and Catholic attitudes toward the Bible. To do so, Puller (like many others since) ended his argument by treating Scripture as a species of objective data—cut loose from ecclesial history, sanctified tradition, and the Holy Spirit's life. This was a typical move. In fact, the reasonable study of Scripture, so desired by Christians wearied of the interminable and irresolvable debates of their coreligionists, quite deliberately placed its interpretive fate in the hands of well-rested and intestinally quiescent scholars. If not repudiated outright, the fundamentally theological character of Scripture was at least deliberately shunted aside as a result of Puller's and others' almost political interest in affirming an ecclesial ground that could disenfranchise religious groups on both the Protestant and Catholic margins.

In contrast to this politicized and thoroughly modern notion of the moderated mean, the center of the Church's theological focus has had a venerably alternative and nonhorizontal construal within the tradition. Here the concept of center has taken on the personalized image of divine integration, described through what could be called a "geometry of force." Augustine, in his parsing of Psalm 46:4–5, gives a typical example of this traditional sense of center. "There is a river whose streams make glad the city of God," writes the Psalmist, "the holy habitation of the Most High. God is in the midst [*in media*] of her, she shall not be moved, God will help her right early." "*In media*" here, Augustine insists, refers to the very life of God's being as it exists in an equidistant creative power and love with respect to all of creation, manifested with revelatory and redeeming clarity in the city of the Church of Christ. To speak of a center is to speak of the eternally orchestrating power of God's own life as it withstands temporal assaults, orders the world, and moves the Church's destiny, all the while maintaining its integrity in relation to every detail of creation. Therefore, another way to describe this same divine center is by the personal name "Jesus, the Messiah."

Translating this traditional figure into a more formally two-dimensional image, we could think of the theological center as a point that wields the power to define a circumference. A center requires the initiating and punctilious bite of the compass, as well as the sweeping action of definition. The area created, in turn, coheres only by consistent reference back to its originating point, thereby defining this wider zone of expansive yet bounded life. But "point," "sweep," and "coherence" are not separable within the creation of a circle; they form, rather, the single body that enwraps the existence of centrality. To say that something in the Christian faith is central, then, is to imply a coherent and complex act, even a kind of life. Christian centrality is less defined by discrete propositional commitments than by a process of discursively articulating and enacting divine realities within ongoing practices of corporate discipline and mission. To speak of Christian centralities is to affirm the creative, particular, and historically encompassing life of God as temporally drawn in the figure of Jesus, the Christ.

The theological center of the Christian faith with respect to Scripture, in particular, derives from this notion of centrality, and actually informs it. To apprehend the center with respect to Scripture will involve grasping Scripture's role within the divinely integrative act that orders creation through the history of Jesus. Scripture, in this sense, forms the "medium" (not the "mean") of God's creative and coherent sweep in the midst of the world through Jesus Christ. Therefore, the Church's self-definition at the theological center with respect to Scripture must mean this: **the whole Church will again hear the voice of the one Lord Jesus in the whole Scripture as she subjects herself to Scripture's integral form.**

We must endeavor to understand the preceding sentence as a single thought, to understand it in such a way that its components cohere. For only then can we safely exegete the implications of its message.

First, **the whole Church**—that is, the Church intentionally bound together through its own disparities of membership, and that seeks to hear with common ears—will hear the Scripture in such a way that both the common Church and the single Scripture are brought together (not treated as discrete objective and subjective entities).

Second, the Church hears the **entire Scripture**, both the Old and New

Testaments together. The distinctness of the coming of Jesus Christ and its dependence upon God's covenant with Israel are bound in the common implication of full Christological and Trinitarian affirmations. It is, after all, the voice of Jesus Christ that the whole Scripture speaks, though in distinct ways that must be brought into some coherent focus. In turn, the confession and coherence implied in this hearing point to the fact that the testaments are heard as Scripture, divinely authorized in their collective shaping as canon.

Finally, the Church hears this Scripture even now, **again and again.** Thereby it loses neither the necessity of a preceding and surrounding tradition of hearing—the "common ears" of the body whose unity is temporal as well and geographical—nor the need to hear again, occasioned by the state of endangerment into which that tradition may fall. Only through this consistent historical self-mooring in the tradition can the Church subject itself to the integral form of Scripture, constantly binding itself to the comprehensive power of the word. Hearing within the ordered "sweep" of the Church's temporal life demands that the Church neither reject what it cannot just now understand nor assume that what is just now understood in part must stand for the whole.

In this perspective, the Church's theological center with respect to Scripture has a regulative character, not a compromising one. Boundaries given in the realities of coherence and integrity—testamentally, temporally, geographically, and referentially—constantly assert themselves as the Church orders its life within the grasp of Scripture's whole, which reflects the single and sweeping act of God's creative life in Jesus Christ. The Church is constantly pushed and limited by the medium of this divine act embodied by Scripture.

Although regulative in this sense, the center's reality is also given historically, as a process of constant "reapprehension" within those geographic and temporal strains that constitute the Church's commonality with respect to membership, and even to Scripture's force. "God is in the midst of her," Psalm 46 asserts; yet this creative center takes shape as the Church itself lives in the midst of a "changing earth," "shaking mountains," and "tumultuous" waters and times (verses 2–3), which the Psalm describes. The center is God's ordering life, not the Church, which must suffer the flux of the present in its opaque swirl. It is because the Scripture functions regulatively within the historically strained traditions of the Church that the

Church is a body *semper reformanda*—always recreated in the image of the ordering whole, and always articulating the saving bonds of God's work described in Scripture.

One significant implication of conceiving the vital theological center of the Church in this way pertains directly to this volume's attempt to think "creedally," even as, and precisely because, its authors have sought to think in terms of an integrally whole and authoritative Scripture. Both Scripture and the creed have suffered dismemberment at the hands of modern criticism. These essays seek to describe this plight and overcome it. Scriptural canon (as addressed in the talks of Professor Childs) and ecclesial creed (as it informs the concerns of the accompanying speakers) are understood to form together a single, inseparable, and irreplaceable approach to Scripture as it stands at the center of the Church's life.

One of the most telling signs of the vitality of this commitment is the way it now forcefully (and in a somewhat novel way) informs Professor Childs's response to contemporary debunkers of the Bible. This response consists, according to Childs, in a retrieval of traditional modes of exegesis that critical biblical scholarship would simply have deemed unworthy of scrutiny only a few years ago. In a manner that is completely consistent (in commitment, if not necessarily in execution) with this bold orientation, the present essays on the creed adopt its traditional significance, by focusing on its phrases, as a rule for the reading of Sripture.

There are a number of notable aspects to this inseparability of the canon and creed of Scripture. Firstly, we can identify what might be termed their historical-genetic linkage. In the late second century A.D. there emerged, as a response to the early Church'e life-or-death struggle with Gnosticism, the formalization of the authority of both the canon and the baptismal creeds as a "rule of faith" (*regula fidei*). In historical terms, the scriptural canon and creed are joined at the hip. This is a well-worn critical observation, although it has rarely been faced squarely in the modern era as an inescapable theological datum.

In itself, however, this purely historical linkage does not suffice to demonstrate the necessary theological connection between canon and creed in the present. Therefore, we must note secondly how contemporary analyses of the Church, with the help of sociological and anthropological tools, have emphasized the distinctiveness of the connection. They have pointed out that our reading of the biblical text as Scripture is based on a decision made by the Church that these writings should function in this way. Both canon and creed as rules (*regulae*) serve to define that function. Those who fail to understand their connected role cannot grasp their respective and common importance.

This socio-anthropological appeal, if taken alone, could obviously lend itself to the misapprehension that the Church arbitrarily wills its linguistic and theological life to be played out by these scriptural and creedal rules. Many conservative and liberal critics of a postliberal theology stressing the culturally constructive character of religion have pointed this out. In our postmodern climate, such an affirmation of the socially arbitrary drifts easily into a kind of ecclesiological voluntarism that is quite alien to the theological ancestry behind the view that sees canon and creed as mutually informing rules. Although the arguments for canon and creed's inseparability, taken from history and function, are true, they are not in themselves sufficient.

Third, a more narrowly theological dimension to the linkage of canon and creed needs to be stressed, for their historically and functionally connective character serves to remind us that we err if we start with each— Scripture as canon and creed as the rule for Scripture's reading— understood as two entities that must be unstably tethered together. The Christian perspective, properly understood, always begins with a single and coherent action that defines the circumference of the Christian's practical and intellectual world: the center. This center is found in the explication of the scriptural material itself, whose sweep is governed by its organizing form. In other words, the coherence we speak of grows out of the coherence internal to the scriptural witness. As Professor Childs has rigorously and passionately argued, Jesus Christ is himself the center of the Old, as well as the New, Testament witness. The Church, therefore, in its extended historical story of faith and faithlessness, is already present in that scriptural witness as an instrumental testimonial. In connecting canon and creed, the answer to any suspicion of arbitrariness is thus given in the affirmation of divine providence—in the "geometry of force"—which is given in the self-ordering of God in created time, and takes the form of Christ himself as he draws Israel and the Church together in his person. (A famous rendering of this case can be found in Michael Ramsey's ecclesiological classic, *The Gospel and the Christian Church*. In our volume, George Sumner's discussion of the Ascension's historical character points to the concrete geo-ecclesial implications of the world's providential ordering within the bounded forms of Scripture's reference.)

In this light, coherence stands as a consistent theme throughout the essays of this volume; their authors are continually at work to repair those intellectual dualisms, born of modernity, that so lend themselves to the disintegrative opposite of coherence. Christopher Seitz, for instance, shows how one can only understand who Jesus is once one perceives how inseparable his identity is from the promises of God given to Israel. Because of this coherence between Old Testament promises and the New Testament messianic history, any notion of a historical Jesus filtered out from the environment of scripturally inscribed promise and fulfilment must be untrue to Jesus in himself. Or again, Ephraim Radner uncovers the originally apprehended coherence between Scripture, Church, and history, which was both the premise and the proof of traditional apologetics. Stephen Holmgren, for his part, argues for a wider coherence between the doctrines of creation and redemption, and for a coherence between our moral and spiritual lives and the pattern of that redeemed creation. And Russell Reno, in addressing the scriptural and creedal assertion of redemption, claims that a perception of Scripture as authoritative must be bound inseparably to the conversion of the heart.

These are all fairly traditional arguments in themselves. However, their conjunction brings into peculiar relief the Christian affirmation that derives such variegated expressions of coherence from the fundamental reality that God is properly God as he exercises his power to hold together the life of creation, human and ecclesial history, and redemption within his own self. At the center of God's creative sweep is the living form of Jesus, the Christ, the Father's Son. One may disdain faith in such a God, but one cannot claim that this God, whose life founds these coherent forms, is not the Christian God. The commitment to coherence as the expression of the Christian center is of a basic theological—not merely logical—order.

In this volume, we present essays that respond to a number of contemporary concerns, but we deliberately order them so as to reflect the tradition's understanding of who Jesus Christ is. So, first of all, we have offered Professor Childs' essay on the Lordship of Christ, witnessed to in the Scriptures of the Church, under the rubric of "The Character of the Divine Christ," and have arrayed alongside it essays addressing His eternal Sonship and His Role as Creator. We have followed the logic of the creed by moving next to "The Historical Reality of Jesus the Christ," so that modern historical problems about who Jesus is are addressed, but in the light of traditional ways of hearing Scripture, and with the aid of the doctrines of the incarnation and the atonement. Finally, under the creedal rubrics of Christ's resurrection, ascension, and return, in a section subtitled "The Lordship of Jesus Christ in Human History," we include essays that widen our sense of "history" that is Jesus', to include such dimensions as the history of Israel, the story of the Church's missionary expansion, and the final judgment on all human culture. Ordering our essays with the creedal mind of the Church, and weaving together interpretive and dogmatic essays, aiming throughout to recast the questions our time asks of Jesus, we have sought a form fit to the coherence we deem necessary to the Christian theological task.

Schooling in theological coherence, then, must precede and follow the hearing of biblical texts as Scripture for the Christian Church. The essays in this volume may be seen simply as moments within this process of Christian pedagogy, but we must perceive various kinds of conditions as upholding this schooling. There is the formal condition, that we be in the kind of Church that supposes it has a Scripture to hear; there is a material condition, that we can truly discern the contents of this Scripture itself; and there is the moral condition, that we ourselves, as the Church, possess the virtues of attentiveness and humility to accomplish such discernment. Each of these conditions needs to inform the practice of the whole Church in hearing the voice of the Lord Jesus Christ in the entirety of Scripture and in subjecting itself to this word. But it is possible to speak to these conditions in distinctive ways, precisely since they represent necessarily emphasized aspects in a process of applied discipline.

Any seeming tension in approach among the essays' authors results from such distinctive reflection on particular disciplines. These tensions, however, are actually superficial, since each approach is presupposed as contributing to the formation of a coherent and integral hearing by the whole Church. A canonical approach like that of Professor Childs focuses on the material conditions for retrieving the center: The integrity of both testaments must be preserved, the hermeneutical center of all reading is the Lord Jesus Christ, and the reader of Scripture must refer all discourse in a realist manner to God (as opposed, for example, to human religious consciousness or to intracommunal sign-systems). By contrast, some postliberal theologians (notably George Lindbeck, under whom several of the present contributors studied) have emphasized formal conditions for retrieval, especially a recognition of how Scripture functions within the Church, an understanding of the nature of a reading's tradition, a community formation through language, and so forth. One might also note the concern of some of the essayists for the moral conditions undergirding the apprehension and reception of the scriptural center, concerns that reflect in part the influence of ethicists like Stanley Hauerwas and John Howard Yoder. But the distinctive emphases of scholars such as Childs, Lindbeck, or Hauerwas do not stand in a contradictory relationship, certainly not as they are exhibited in the intentional purposes of this collection of essays. Rather, they presuppose each other in their respective collaborative and formative roles, themselves cohering in the common endeavor of drawing the circle of faith from the theological center that Scripture embodies.

If we can see how these conditions are distinct but complementary, we can also perceive, by contrast, how ideologically charged are the alternatives that today claim critical or anticritical status as standard-bearers for our particular historical moment. Fundamentalism and pure historical criticism are not simply two poles that may call for a mediating mean on the part of the ecclesially pacific. They are rather two critical perspectives of which each derives from a common foreshortening of the Church's reality that is, as we have seen, properly correlative with that of Scripture. Connected with this, each denies, in a basic way, the creative and ordering force of divine providence as the sweeping center of the temporal world in which Scripture's life is given in the Church's own ambiguous history. Subverted, then, are both formal and material conditions for the hearing of Scripture as the center's communicative medium.

More vague liberal formulas currently applied to Scripture's hearing (which see the value of a biblical text as lying in its capacity to promote "imaginative" conversation or to uncover the "voices of the marginal") also neglect the material condition by skirting the theological task of relating the circumference back to the Christian faith's center. The moral condition for hearing is severely compromised in such formulas, as humility and patience before that divine center are relativized in favor of a search for more truncated objects of attention.

Thus, in contrast to the view of Church and Scripture espoused in this volume, the alternate views are characterized by a lack of coherence between Church and Scripture, and between the virtues required for true hearing and the subject matter of Scripture itself. Where this coherence is lacking, the resulting positions, whether of a liberal or a conservative stripe, invariably take on an ideological tinge as they assert some orienting perspective that is now cut loose from the encompassing center we have been describing. Ideology is not simply an imbalance; it is the creation, by default usually, of a new compass with a different point of origin and a constricted sweep.

When we view the alternatives to the theological center in this light, we attain a new perspective on the very nature of criticism. This volume claims to consider canon and creed in a "critical age"—the term by which the modern age, by virtue of its dominant intellectual hardware, has customarily been characterized. However, as we have hinted at various points in this introduction, sheer historical criticism may more fairly be considered anticritical in the sense that it provides so little distance from or purchase on its cultural surroundings and their presuppositions. The critiques to which these essays respond have acquired a rote quality.

By way of shorthand, we can observe that our critical age has been built on historical relativism, a hermeneutic of suspicion about the motives behind traditional claims, and an assumption of the autonomous individual, freed from authority and community. But it is in the light of the theological center that varieties of history are drawn together. In that same light a more searching critique of motives yet can be offered, and, by contrast, a life of practices conducing to an end beyond what one could have previously imagined. The supposedly critical age turns out to be a pallid reflection of the life inscribed by the center.

For this reason, a number of our essayists find critical purchase on both Church life and the larger society emerging from the heart of Christian doctrine itself. One may look back to the precedent of Barth, whose turn to a Christocentric eschatology, far from hermetically closing off his theology, opened the way for an incisive critique of his intellectual and theological milieu. In this respect, several of our contributors may be seen as Barth's grandchildren. Kathryn Greene-McCreight offers a critique of feminist Christological arguments by appealing to a Christocentric eschatology and, in so doing, points out a more fruitful avenue for a legitimate Christian feminism. Kendall Harmon insists that preaching focussed on the coming Christ leads to true human transformation. Christopher Brown rejects a culturally compromised reading of incarnation in favor of a more interventionist understanding that is capable of addressing us with words of judgment and grace. Finally, William Witt speaks on behalf of all such arguments when he counsels theology to eschew facile appeals to some general notion of symbol, and to cleave to the narrative witness in its particularity, from which has flown a rich profusion of expressions of that single, saving work. There the Judge was judged and mercy pronounced on our age too—and therein theology from the center proves itself truly critical.

Ultimately, the real test is whether or not these essays, in their course, can demonstrate the coherence of which we speak, as they attempt to read Scripture, as part of the interpretive tradition, in the face of modernity's challenges. How, for instance, might we characterize the present (and highly concrete) debate within mainline churches over the proper shape of ecclesial organization, worship, and ministry that has been raised by the well-publicized numerical success of "megachurch" strategies? Although topics such as sexuality drive church conventions and resolutions, the issue of church organization and expression, which is creating a wealth of new models eagerly grasped after by desperate church leaders, is arguably of far more consequence to the Church's future. Many aspects of the new church-growth and megachurch strategies have explicit theological substance, despite their market-driven origins, and should be examined carefully—that is, critically within a coherent framework of faith, in order to be properly assessed.

For example, from the start the deliberate excision of whole swathes from these strategies of scriptural witness and historical Church testimony ought to render immediately suspect their ability to meet with integrity (let alone to care about) the conditions for hearing Sripture that undergird life at the gospel's center. When self-fulfillment and personal experience, over against the self-denial of obedience, become the orienting rules for communal Christian existence—as they are in these new strategies of evangelism and growth—it is not just a question of culturally appropriate styles or symbolic emphases that is raised; the actual existence of a gospel center is placed in doubt. As a result, the critical edge of these so-called "new paradigms" for ministry, many of which claim evangelical parentage, is considerably dulled, whatever the sociological sophistication, in comparison with a more integral grasp of the scriptural Church. It is this lack of such an integral grasp by church leaders that has led to an uncritical acceptance of these cultured modes of ecclesial existence.

From the other ideological side of the spectrum we can note the shape of a recent Episcopal decision concerning the nature of core doctrine for the Church. The so-called "Righter Decision" emerged from of an ecclesiastical trial over the ordination of sexually active gay persons. (Bishop Righter was the clergyman accused of having defied church discipline and doctrine through his knowing ordination of an active homosexual.) The decision to acquit Righter displays the almost intentional lurch of incoherence, which derives from a refusal to acknowledge the connective power of Scripture and history. The very image of a core, to which the episcopal tribunal turned in order to decouple supposedly malleable and hence unenforceable disciplinary customs from evangelical truth, precisely demonstrated its distance from the center in proving incapable of exercising any clarifying or regulating function on this contested topic.

In the decision sharp distinctions were drawn between culture and doctrinal essentials, and between social realities or historical developments and the core of Christian doctrine. To be sure, the articulation of the ways in which these elements relate to each other needs to be careful and nuanced. But the elements themselves are located within the single set of conditions that ought to inform "the whole Church hearing the voice of the Lord Jesus in the whole of Scripture and subjecting itself to this." And once the historical aspect of the formal and moral conditions for hearing Scripture were so starkly relativized, as they were in the decision, the entire providential character of the gospel center was alienated from the discussion, and the possibility for Scripture to act as a consistent formative medium in the creative action of God in Christ Jesus was rendered incredible.

The simple assertions of the Apostles' Creed that the decision lifted up as core doctrine, though without explicit behavioral punch, now floated so freely from Scripture, that their historical bite as tied to, for instance, the actual moral teachings of the Law and Jesus, became cultural irrelevancies. The whole subsequent debate following from the trial demonstrated the pinched and constricting character of the decision's decentered and hence ideologically ordered perspective. From the conservative side, we were treated with affirmations of decontextualized scriptural verses that were deployed to reject gay ordinations. From the more liberal side, we were treated with a Scripture that was dissolved into vague moral terms, disembodied from the life of scriptural reference, designed to render such verses irrelevant to Christian doctrine and life itself.

We believe that a rediscovery of the gospel center as we have explained it in relation to Scripture, will prove its transformative value in the midst of these kinds of community reflections and sometimes disputes. But life in the center is just that: It is a life, not only an intellectual analysis. No Gordian knots are cut with respect to besetting quandaries. It would, of course, seem easier and clearer to offer a method or a formula. But on the contrary, we are describing the coherence of a complex text with a community that across history has engaged in various practices in order to render and be conformed to the real presence of Christ. It is difficult to hold onto all of these dimensions at once. They do, in fact, cohere, but only in reference to their center. The practice of indwelling the world in which Scripture is used by God as the ordering form for God's own creative life in Christ Jesus gives rise to a Church whose temporal shape is not provided in advance. The scriptural Church is carried forward by God's Spirit in peculiar and particular ways, whose only predictability is provided in the particularities of Jesus—in word and deed.

What, then would it mean for us to reinhabit this gospel center? Let take a step back and consider a historically longer vista. The moment in which the Church presently stands may best be understood if we compare it with two prominent turning points that have preceded us. At the Reformation, the urgent task was to hear again the Scripture, and Jesus Christ as Lord at its center. Martin Luther believed that he was addressing this task in his whole theological and reforming endeavor. This is not the occasion for an assessment of his revolt, but we can observe that "hearing the Scripture again" for Luther meant achieving some distance from the preceding tradition of interpretation that had contributed to its obscurement. By contrast, renewal of faith at the beginning of the Oxford movement, in the early nineteenth century—so important for modern Anglicans—involved a conscious turning back to and retrieval of explicitly Church doctrine, its tradition and authority.

And now? Our moment is again one that must hear the Scripture anew—as much as in the sixteenth century. But we who must relearn this hearing of the Scripture must do so by cleaving to the whole Church, thinking and living with it, and relearning its tradition of interpretation. This is a profoundly critical task, engaging faculties of analysis, historical insight, ethical acumen, and resistance, brought together in a coherent apprehension of God's life in Christ Jesus for the world. In the face of the many accepted and often celebrated incoherences of contemporary culture, rehearing the whole Scripture with the tradition of and as the whole Church in the entirety of God's creative time will mean rendering ourselves strange and suspicious with respect to the fragmented customs of our surrounding world. Modern popular and intellectual atittudes have long treated the Scripture with suspicion although they have found nothing there that lay beyond the scattered scraps of text. A critical faith, a faith at the center, which this volume commends, will now adopt this same suspicious stance toward the disintegrated flailings of a forgetful culture, not so much to deconstruct this culture into further fragments as to look back at what has been forgotten: the single, full, scripturally inscribed embrace with which God, in Jesus, has taken up our history.

Section One

The Character of the Divine Christ

Jesus Christ the Lord and the Scriptures of the Church

The Reverend Dr. Brevard S. Childs

The Sources of the Present Confusion

It is not my intention to review in detail the many recent attempts to reconstruct a new portrait of Jesus. These efforts of creating a new understanding in accord with modern cultural norms are not new. In Albert Schweitzer's classic volume, *The Quest of the Historical Jesus* (1906), he has given an exhaustive account of the history of various proposals from the late eighteenth through the nineteenth centuries.

What characterized the nineteenth-century effort was the confidence that by using the correct historical-critical method one could penetrate through the canonical Gospels and recover a more rational and appealing figure. It was first thought that if one simply removed the supernatural elements, an accessible portrait matching ordinary human experience would emerge. Then a proposal was developed contending that if the different literary strands were critically rearranged—Mark being the earliest gospel and John designated as late and unreliable—a very new historical figure would emerge. Then, in 1835, a dramatic shift took place in the field of New Testament with the publication of David Friedrich Strauss's book, *The Life of Jesus Critically Examined*. Strauss argued that all the sources of the New Testament were affected by a mythical consciousness through which the gospel material had been filtered, and that this consciousness largely absorbed all historical memory into a tendentious human construct. By the end of the nineteenth century it had become evident that the quest for a critically reconstructed Jesus of history had been a failure and that the subjective and philosophically prejudicial dimension had increased rather than diminished.

Yet, in all fairness, it would be wrong to conclude that the whole effort had been a total loss. The intense scrutiny of the Gospels did point out the strikingly different voices of the four evangelists, which up to that time had not been sufficiently recognized. In addition, the critical effort did much to destroy the traditional method of easy harmonization of the gospels, which often had been equally as rationalistic as the nineteenth-century liberal critics.

The nineteenth-century critical approaches continued to be represented well into the twentieth century, especially in the English-speaking world. For example, in 1927 Shirley Jackson Case, a professor of New Testament at Chicago, wrote a new biography of Jesus that exploited recent sociological theories of religion and society. Also, in some respects, Rudolf Bultmann's early 1929 volume on Jesus, which was published in a popular series titled "The Immortals," was a continuation of the nineteenth century's literary critical reductionism. The effect of the philosophical dissolution stemming from World War I was already evident in Bultmann's move from the lovable, idealistic figure of Harnack to that of an existentialist who called for concrete decisions in the face of life's tragic imponderables. In the decades following World War II most of Bultmann's students avoided writing lives of Jesus. The few tentative probes of Bornkamm, Käsemann, and Conzelmann were pale and hesitant attempts to escape the nineteenth-century critical legacy with all of its obvious failures.

In light of this brief review, how then is one to explain the recent explosion of new interest in a so-called "Third Quest for the Historical Jesus"? It is not by accident that the movement is strongest in the English-speaking world, especially in the United States. I have been struck by the fact that many of its proponents—E. P. Sanders, Marcus Borg, and John Shelby Spong, to name a few—have come out of conservative, even fundamentalist, backgrounds. In his several books on the search which come across as quite pious in tone, Borg genuinely tries to encourage a type of religious faith by creating a more politically correct, mystical Jesus that immediately resonates with a certain segment of American culture. Even the radical, avant-garde Roman Catholic scholar J. D. Crossan cannot be construed as antiecclesiastical, but rather as one who is offering a very different option as a substitute for traditional Christianity. None of these scholars are out to trash the importance of religion as a cultural phenomenon. Rather, the adversary is always traditional Christian orthodoxy, both catholic and evangelical.

A variety of factors are involved that have shaped the new quest. First, the appeal to sociological forces as a dominant influence in determining the form of the Christian religion is everywhere presupposed. This approach seeks to determine the cultural roots of Jewish, Hellenistic, and sectarian groups out of which Christianity arose and from which its religious experience was shaped. Moreover, the modern discoveries at Qumran and Nag Hammadi have encouraged this emphasis as sharper profiles of gnostic, ecstatic, and apocalyptic groups have been constructed. A frequent corollary of this interest, which goes back to Reimarus and Lessing, is that these creative forces have been layered over and constrained by a later ecclesiastical construct, largely self-serving, that has increasingly misunderstood the true significance of Jesus. According to this model, a major goal is to replace the early Church's misunderstanding by a more accurate, sociological picture. Discursive speech is understood largely as the formation of images, whose function is construed as identity-building in nature. This move allows the interpreter to seek modern analogies to communal functions without normative doctrinal ballast. Thus, Wayne Meeks can translate the Pauline language of justification and eschatology into a process of resocialization within the context of friendship.

A second major influence has joined the sociological approach with a more radical, postmodern philosophical understanding of textual meaning as indeterminate, a never-ending pursuit of open-ended tropes. Meaning does not cohere to any determinate form of a text, but is acquired only through the reading process that produces literary sense. There is no privileged context assigned to the apostolic witness of the New Testament, but the context of the reader shapes a meaning within certain communal restraints. This hermeneutical theory accounts for the endless variety of diverse readings: Marxist, ethnic, feminist, and psychological.

Another factor is the influence of so-called "narrative theology." Much good and illuminating has come from some of its advocates. The recovery of the Bible as a coherent story served to overcome the nineteenth-century fragmentation of the texts into bits and pieces. Narrative theology was also very helpful in forcing the interpreter to seek to hear all the nuances of each text in its own right, within a larger literary whole without concentrating immediately on academic questions of historicity. Hans Frei's famous book, *The Eclipse of Biblical Narrative* (1974), freed an entire scholarly generation from its preoccupation with questions of external referentiality by showing the great variety within the Bible's own rendering of theological intertextuality.

Yet, almost immediately scholars began to understand the Bible as a story in purely literary categories, without any serious concern for its theological content. When Karl Barth first spoke about the "strange new world of the

Bible," he was speaking of the world of God. In modern narrative theology the Bible has increasingly become a story by which every form of human aspiration and alternative visions of an ideal society are projected through creative imagination. God's story was replaced with "our story" as once again theology was turned into anthropology.

Recently, viewers had the chance to watch the numerous television programs chaired by Bill Moyers on the book of Genesis. On initially hearing of this project, I had a very positive reaction and greeted with expectation the discussions of a battery of serious and educated readers. I assumed, rather naively, that any reading of the Bible must be of value. I quickly became deeply disappointed as week after week the participants raised, in my judgment, all the wrong questions, immediately becoming mired in the murky waters of skepticism, personal alienation, and psychological paralysis. The clear witness of God's many ways of dealing with his rebellious creation turned into a cacophony of misunderstanding and human hubris. It reminded me of the Garden of Eden and the serpent's query: "Did God really say . . . ?" In the end, I felt that all the deep problems of the modern quest for God in American society were writ large for all to see in their painful confusion.

The Role of the Bible as Sacred Scripture

The present confusion regarding Jesus Christ is derived in large measure from the failure to understand the nature of the Scripture that bears testimony to him. How one conceives the Bible directly affects how one views the Christ. If Scripture is not regarded as a vehicle of truthful witness, but instead as a faulty filtering prism through which the person of Jesus has been impaired or severely distorted, then by necessity one must find another access to this figure. This assumption, I submit, ultimately lies at the heart of the present confusion as different proposals regarding Jesus are articulated: the ascetic mystic, the political radical, the eschatological fanatic, or the cool Kissinger-like sage, expounding wise aphorisms or expedient counsel.

The question of the Church's understanding of Scripture entails a variety of both historical and theological issues. Among the central points in this understanding and shaping of Scripture is that Jesus' first disciples were all Jews. They were loyal to the God of Israel, whom they worshiped in the temple and in their synagogues. They lived from the revelation of God to his chosen people, as contained in the Hebrew Scriptures. During their lives with Jesus they were constantly being instructed in the divine word: "Search the Scriptures for they speak of me" (John 6:39).

For at least one hundred years after the resurrection, the Jewish Scriptures served as the only Bible of the Church. Yet it was clear from the beginning that the early Christians shared a different approach than their Jewish contemporaries to these sacred writings. The Church's language of faith was not tied to the Hebrew language as was rabbinic Judaism, but almost immediately the Greek, Latin, and Coptic languages were used to communicate the gospel. Certainly the biblical text was considered sacred, but this was because of the divine content to which it bore witness. The biblical text in itself was not a reality-creating entity, but rather the Holy Spirit brought life to the word to reveal its living testimony to Jesus as the Christ. In spite of Bishop Spong's recent discovery of Jewish midrash as holding the key to the New Testament, in point of fact, midrashic exegesis was at best a peripheral phenomenon within Christianity. The issue for the church was that of theological substance and not of literary techniques. Second Peter states this conviction succinctly, "We did not follow cleverly devised myths when we made known to you the power and coming of our Lord Jesus Christ, but we were eyewitnesses of his majesty . . . and we have the prophetic word made sure" (1:16–19).

Very shortly, along with the written Jewish Scriptures, the stories from and about Jesus were collected and, within thirty years, were formed into written gospels. For a time, both oral and written forms of the gospel coexisted. This was made clear when attacks on the Church's teaching arose from the Gnostics, who constructed a very different, esoteric portrait of Jesus. In the second century the Catholic Church, under the leadership of men like Irenaeus, responded by appealing to a rule of faith (*regula fidei*). This was not simply a baptismal formula, as thought in the nineteenth century, but it was a core of Christian belief on which the Christian faith was grounded, the one catholic tradition expressed in both oral and written form. There was only one Gospel, but it was testified to by Matthew, Mark, Luke, and John. It is important to emphasize that when the four Gospels were deemed canonical—authoritative for faith and practice—they were not rendered normative by an ecclesial power imposed from the top down. Rather, in their use by diverse Christian congregations and from the coercion of the evangelical witness itself, their authority was recognized and acknowledged as from God.

One of the earliest crises of the Church came in the middle of the second century when it became increasingly evident that the Scriptures of the Old Testament, even when read as the law of Christ, were not adequate or complete without being supplemented by a written evangelical witness—the New Testament. One can sense even from the shape of the Gospels the impending crisis that ultimately led to the formation of the second testament. Luke's prologue uses language reflecting the consciousness that the form of the witness to the gospel was no longer that of original eyewitnesses, but was being set down in written form by later traditions. A new medium for truthful proclamation was called for as the first generation of eyewitnesses began to die. Using the literary conventions of Hellenistic rhetoric, Luke expresses his intention to write an orderly account "that you may know the truth concerning the things you have heard" (1:4).

What finally emerged was a Christian Bible that consisted of an Old Testament and a New Testament, both witnessing to Jesus Christ, the old testifying in terms of prophecy, and the new of fulfillment. Yet both speak of the future eschatological rule of God. The Christian Bible was formed from two different collections, each having its discrete traditional history, but together comprising the one unified testimony to God in Jesus Christ.

The precise date the New Testament took a definitive shape has been much discussed. The term *New Testament* appears in Irenaeus and becomes common soon thereafter. The present reigning hypothesis, first established in the late nineteenth century by patristic giants such as Zahn and Harnack, argues that the formation of the completed New Testament was the result of a long and rather tortuous process extending over several centuries. It was thought that there was a basic canonical corpus by the end of the second century that consisted of the four Gospels and most of the letters of Paul. However, only by the end of the fourth century did the other parts of the New Testament—Acts, General Epistles, and Revelation—assume canonical status. This position was essentially the view I defended in my book *The New Testament as Canon*, which was written twelve years ago.

Recently there have been some exciting new studies on the subject. I mention, above all, the brilliant book of David Trobisch, titled *The Final Redaction of the New Testament: An Investigation of the Formation of the Christian Bible*, which is to appear in an English translation from Oxford University Press. Trobisch is convinced that there is new evidence to show that there already was a definitive edition of the entire New Testament by the end of the second century. He makes his case on the following evidence.

First, a study of all the manuscript evidence through the seventh century shows the presence of a peculiar system of abbreviating a series of divine names: God, Lord, Jesus, Christ, Spirit, Father, and Son. (Trobisch calls these *nomina sacra*.) He argues that these abbreviations are unique to the Christian Bible and that they show the early dating of an actual literary publication of an edition of the entire New Testament in codex form, whether written in capital or minuscule letters.

Furthermore, the titles of authorship assigned to each of the writings—those of Matthew, Mark, Luke, John, Paul, James, Peter, and Jude—are consciously intertwined throughout the entire New Testament to show an inner-referentiality, and thus to form a unified authoritative whole. For example, Mark is linked in Acts with both Paul and Peter and he also is greeted in the letter of 1 Peter. Luke likewise is referred to in the Gospels, Acts, and the Pauline collection, and is linked with Mark. John is named in the Fourth Gospel, the synoptics, Acts, and Revelation. Similarly, the General Epistles are consciously linked through cross-referencing to James, Peter, and John. The effect is that a knowledge of the whole New Testament corpus emerges as an actual literary force in shaping once independent writings into a unified composition.

Finally, the conflict between Peter and Paul, referred to in the letter to the Galatians, is brought to a conscious harmonious end in Acts 15. Likewise, Paul and James are joined in a shared plan in Acts 21 to unite Jewish and Gentile Christians in a common collection for Jerusalem. In fact, the major function of the book of Acts is to provide an introduction to the Catholic Epistles and the historical background for the Pauline letters. It also is not accidental that in the last letters of both Paul and Peter the public reading of Scripture within the community of faith is highly commended.

I confess that I have not yet fully digested Trobisch's hypothesis, nor do I understand fully its implications. However, I mention this daring thesis to illustrate a fresh turn in New Testament studies, long overdue, of seeking to understand the nature of the Church's search for a holistic and unified grasp of its Scriptures. Most of the scholarly energy of the New Testament guild has focused on historical or literary reconstructions apart from the received form of our New Testament. Trobisch has opened up a fresh vista in showing at what early date the Church may have been dealing with a written corpus of authoritative Scripture with its witness to the one Gospel of Jesus Christ.

Theological Implications Derived from the Church's Canon

There are several implications that stem from the fact of an authoritative canon. As I have tried to show, the formation of the Christian Bible involved both historical and theological problems that were always closely intertwined. Both dimensions are equally important in today's debate in interpreting the Bible.

For example, Elaine Pagels argues that the Christian Bible served as a propaganda document devised by a small sect that constructed it largely out of whole cloth in order to further its own private agenda. One can easily refute such an outrageous theory, however, by appealing to the historical formation of the biblical corpus. Its shaping involved a host of decisions, extending over at least 150 years, in which the Church's tradition through constant use of the corpus was preserved, transmitted, and celebrated in public. A major factor distinguishing the formation of the Catholic tradition from that of Gnosticism was that the process was not done in secret or controlled by a small conventicle of like-minded zealots.

In another example, Marcus Borg claims to acknowledge the religious attraction of the truly historical Jesus, which has been badly blurred and distorted through tendentious transmission. One must reply to such claims: the Jesus we worship is not some elusive figure lost from view and needing the skill of modern critical scholars to recover, but the Christ plainly revealed on every page of the Gospels. It was the lasting contribution of Martin Kähler, professor of New Testament at Halle, to have seen and stated correctly both the historical and theological dimensions of the modern critical debate. His formulation is classic and should be sounded loudly once again. He wrote: "The reason we commune with the Jesus of our Gospels is because it is through them that we learn to know that same Jesus whom we meet at the right hand of God...he is God's revelation to us" (p. 60 f.). "The risen Lord is not the historical Jesus *behind* the Gospels, but the Christ of the Apostolic preaching, of the *whole* New Testament...this real Jesus is the Christ who is proclaimed. The Christ who is preached is, however, precisely the Christ of faith. He is the Jesus whom the eyes of faith behold at every step he takes and through every syllable he utters 'our risen, living Lord'" (p. 65 f.) (*The So-called Historical Jesus and the Historic Biblical Christ*, Philadelphia: Fortress Press, 1964).

I am not suggesting that to accept the canonical Gospels as authoritative resolves all of the problems regarding the New Testament. Far from it! However, the acknowledgment of the Bible as authoritative Scripture provides the correct theological context for its understanding. It sets the stage for its faithful interpretation. From a hermeneutical perspective this is crucial for a number of important reasons.

For one, the term *Scripture* describes the Bible's true content, the revelation of God through Jesus Christ. The Bible in its fully human form is not a projection of the religious aspirations of mankind, but its subject is God.

Secondly, the Bible is a particular kind of literature. It was not written to satisfy human curiosity or to evoke religious speculation on heavenly mysteries, but it is a call for faithful response during one's whole life. In the Gospel accounts, whenever Jesus was asked a speculative question or one evoked by detached curiosity, he flatly rejected it as of no interest. What he instead addressed are the issues of the heart, and of life and death. Jesus turned away all religious pretensions with a sharp imperative: "You are the good neighbor" (Luke 10:36). He confronted his hearers with the presence of a holy God demanding a just response: "Go and do likewise" (Luke 10:37).

Finally, the Bible is the book of the Church, not that the Church owns the Bible, but rather its understanding requires a stance of expectation, an awaiting for divine illumination. For this reason, the preacher traditionally begins the reading of Scripture with the challenge: "Hear the word of God." Surely it is cloaked in human form, yet the promise and the mystery are that through this form God speaks in mercy and in judgment.

Martin Luther told a story of the man who died and awoke before the heavenly tribunal. When condemned for his refusal to accept God's salvation, the man objected: "I never heard any word from God. No one ever gave me a chance to believe." God replied: "I spoke to you every Sunday morning." The man responded: "All I ever heard were the ramblings of an ignorant preacher babbling away." God replied to this: "Precisely, it was I speaking to you in human form the eternal words of life."

In conclusion, the canonical Scriptures establish the proper context for hearing the divine word. They demand much from their listeners: to await the coming of the Spirit and to be transformed through God's gracious gift of salvation.

The Exegetical Challenge of Interpreting Scripture

The acknowledgment of the Bible as the Church's authoritative guide provides the proper context for its interpretation. Yet a variety of difficult, hermeneutical problems remain. What does a given text mean? How does one deal with the great variety of different voices? Is there really a unity of content between the two testaments, the writings of which spanned centuries, with numerous authors addressing different audiences within different periods of time? These problems have become especially acute with the rise of modern historical criticism, which often gives the impression that the modern scientific approach alone is enlightened, and that today's educated readers can take with a grain of salt what does not seem compatible with the cultured way of life.

It is important to recognize that very early in the history of the Christian Church the problem of how to interpret correctly the canonical Scriptures arose. The impulse was for the Church to develop a set of hermeneutical rules for reading its Scriptures, to combat alternative approaches—Gnostic, Docetic, Judaizing—that were judged incompatible with the Church's confession.

Three major figures emerged in the early Church who sought through their writings to guide the Church in its interpretation of Scripture. They are Irenaeus, Origen, and Augustine. Of course there were others involved, but these three stand out for their major contributions. Irenaeus, often called the Father of Christian Orthodoxy, faced in the second century the massive threat from the speculative dualism of Gnosticism that contested the unity of the creation God of Israel and the Father of Jesus Christ. Irenaeus defended the unity of God's salvation, insisting that the two testaments are a harmonious witness to the one redemptive purpose in history. He appealed to the rule of truth (or faith) as a check against the arbitrary exegesis of the Gnostics, and provided a theological framework for scriptural interpretation that acknowledged the truth of the apostolic content in both written and oral tradition.

A generation later, in the third century, Origen sought to deal with the diversity within Scripture by insisting that the Bible should be read according to its multiple levels of meaning. The literal and figurative senses are not two arbitrary levels of meaning, but different forms of divine instruction by means of which the hearer is led from the external form to its internal, spiritual sense. Origen thus sought to read the entire Bible as Christian Scripture and to relate its message to its subject matter, God in the form of the Logos.

Augustine continued to work with the different levels of meaning within Scripture, but he took interpretation out of the realm of isolated literary techniques and grounded it in a holistic rendering of the theological intention. The goal of all Scripture is to engender the love of God and of one's neighbor. Therefore, if a passage, when taken literally, does not refer to this purity of life, it must be understood figuratively and its metaphorical function explored.

Before concluding, I would like to emphasize as strongly as possible the seriousness of the issues before us respecting the authority of the Bible. Perhaps some feel that I have overstated the role of canon and of the Church's particular way of interpreting its Scriptures, but let me raise the stakes by citing another formulation of the Bible's role. This role is one that increasingly has become the accepted approach of large segments of mainline Christianity. This particular statement arises out of the battle presently being waged in the Presbyterian Church over the alleged right to ordain practicing homosexuals. Hal Lloyd, (Network News 16 [1996]:7), writes:

> We Presbyterians have always interpreted the Bible and its confessions contextually, as living writings whose meanings and applications change as the years go by, not rigidly, as dead documents that always mean only what they may have meant to the original writers. We try to discover what they meant to those who wrote them in their time and circumstances, and then try to figure out what they mean to us now in our time and circumstances. That's what all respectable scholarship and preaching are about. We believe that is the only way to come even near to discovering the truth of God for us now, rather than for someone a hundred years or a thousand years ago.

This formulation sets out with great clarity another alternative to the Church's confessional understanding of Scripture under the rubric of "contextualization." It assumes that theologically liberal relativism is the only alternative to naive, rigid literalism. I have attempted to show that there has always been another option, one that provides grounds for the Church's confidence in its Bible as an authoritative guide for faith and practice.

To briefly outline some of the main lines by which the Church sought to establish a faithful reading of its Scriptures: First, the Old and New Testaments together constitute the Christian Bible. The voice of Israel and the voice of the evangelists compose a single narrative of God's redemptive action spanning prophecy and fulfillment. The two testaments are neither to be fused nor separated.

Furthermore, the Bible is to be read according to its literal or plain sense. Its salvific meaning is not esoteric or hidden, but plain and forthright. Careful attention must be paid to its syntax and style. Yet the literal sense is to be balanced by a ruled reading— a reading informed by its subject matter and its confessional content. Augustine's appeal for a reading to engender God's love and love of neighbor is a classic form of a ruled reading.

Thirdly, the Bible contains different levels of meaning, not to be separated, that point to different dimensions of truth and that perform different functions for faith. The form of typology especially extends the meaning of an original event beyond its initial occurrence and finds in it an adumbration of the one consistent purpose of God within history. It provides the Church in each generation with the ability to establish its position in God's plan between salvation already experienced and salvation yet to be consummated.

Finally, the revelation of God in Scripture is the source of the Church's private devotions, communal liturgy, and homiletical instruction. Grounded in the promise that the Holy Spirit will continue to guide each generation of Christians to the final *eschaton*, the people of God await with eager expectation and fervent prayer its fulfillment. *Maranatha,* come quickly Lord Jesus.

We Believe in One Lord, Jesus Christ

Ephraim Radner   *"I believe"*

O
ne of the underlying goals of this volume is to encourage a reflection on the relation between the Lord we confess and believe in and the Jesus whom we study with the tools of historical criticism. Brevard Childs, to whose work I am both responding and bringing critical ecclesial support, has stood at the forefront of Christian scholars who have insisted that there exists a critical unity between these two aspects of Jesus. With force and acuity Childs has exposed some of the troubling implications of our modern ordering of this relation.

My goal here is to concentrate on some of the historical concerns that lie behind this modern "disorder." I do not intend to offer substantive theological articulations of the form and meaning of the Jesus who is both Christ and our Lord. Rather, as a prelude to such articulation, this essay will provide a brief meditation on why our confession of this one Lord, Jesus Christ, seems so incoherent to many today—both outside and of inside the Church. Incoherent not because this person or that person, this group or that group, this church or that church doesn't know what they mean by the confession, but incoherent because they all mean so many different things. It is an irony, felt by many with acute pain, that when we say with the creed, "We believe in one Lord"—in the sense of "one body, one Lord, one faith" (Ephesians 4)—we necessarily contradict ourselves.

I would argue that the historical-critical study of Jesus has been fueled, since its inception in the seventeenth century, in large part by a desire to resolve this incoherence that is rooted at the center of modern Western Christianity. The contemporary marshaling of "historical facts" about Jesus—whether by the orthodox or the unorthodox—represents, I believe, a consistent form of response to an ecclesially untenable diversity of Christian commitments and practices. But because it is a response, the search for the historical grounds of the Christian confession of Jesus as Lord is neither an original cause nor a viable solution to the incoherence itself, which is far more profound than a simple variety of opinions held by otherwise amicably related Christian believers.

In what follows I will give a broad explanation of why the attempt to ground belief in Jesus as Lord on the basis of Jesus' historical factuality arose only in and not before the seventeenth century. In particular, I will try to contrast positively some of the theological and ecclesial realities that made possible the Early Church's noncritical commendation of the faith in Jesus, Messiah and Lord with our own critical but intrinsically inadequate attempts to do so today. And in concluding, I will suggest that our confession in Jesus Christ as the one Lord, however we consider it in orthodox or traditional terms, must be tied to some demanding and probably painful ecclesial practices that will overstep the narrowly theological, and certainly the narrowly political, avenues of vocation to which we have consigned confessional belief in our day.

The historical-critical study of the Bible has peculiar, but very Christian, roots. To take as an example, a well-known contemporary and historical-critically literate commentator on Jesus, Bishop John Spong, has made revisionist efforts at reading the Bible and describing the reality and meaning of Jesus that spring from his deep desire to commend Scripture and his belief in Jesus as the Christ to contemporary people. All of his talk on the Gospels as midrash and his theories about the disciples' projections of their weaknesses and insecurities upon the scriptural record—which many find offensive or compelling, or simply silly—are attempts, as he himself claims, to commend Christianity to a critical, scientifically ordered, pluralistic audience.

Spong, one must note, is an apologist of sorts for the Christian faith. Indeed, most practitioners of the historical-critical study of the Scriptures since the seventeenth century have used their studies apologetically as a primary means of commending a vision of Christian truth. They have been believing Christians, however idiosyncratic, or, if not quite Christian, they have been apologists for a kind of religiosity that might at least embrace Christianity. This is crucial to bear in mind if we are to take accurate stock of the means at our disposal through which we can gain clarity about our confession of Jesus as Lord. Historical-critical examination of the person of Jesus has almost always been offered as an effective tool to come to know this Lord and to persuade others of his reality and significance.

The fact is, however, that it really did not occur to Christians to ground their faith on the critical study of history for almost sixteen hundred years.

This is not to say that Jesus' historical reality was not significant until the post-Reformation. Instead, for sixteen hundred years the establishment of that historical reality was not deemed to be a significant ground for believing in this man as Lord. This really ought to strike us as odd, for it goes against our instinctive grain. Today philosophers argue over whether or not our beliefs need to be "founded" on a certain epistemology; we have arguments over the "Jesus of faith" and the "Jesus of history"; we have debates about the place of "factuality" in the proper interpretation of the Gospels as literary genres. Isn't it odd that we should wait so long for these discussions? Is it simply the case that prior to 1600 all Christians were credulous or superstitious, or, more fashionably, precritical (which sounds suspiciously like uncritical)?

Let us look at the early apologies for Christianity offered in the first centuries of the Church. It is not the case that non-Christians didn't care about the issue of historical fact, and didn't need to be answered on that basis. One has only to read Origen's reply in his work *Contra Celsum (Against Celsus)* to the pagan philosopher Celsus, to realize that Celsus's work, written towards the end of the second century, was filled with exactly the kinds of critical questions that continue to pop up in books by scholars like Spong. In these texts the Gospel accounts are not credible as historical evidence; they represent projections and fabrications by the first Christian community. We can read back through their patina of retrospective justification to discover the "real" Jesus, who was a bastard son of a country slut with a politically unsettling itinerant movement of socially marginal followers, moored to a sectarian Judaism. It appears, from Origen's discussion, that Celsus raised these points, and therefore that people did ask these sorts of questions and give these sorts of answers long before Galileo and Newton. No, the historical questions of modernity are not themselves novel to the period.

Fifty years after Celsus Origen attempted to mount a scattershot response to these kinds of questions. Although he did offer a few critical answers to Celsus' interpretations, it is striking that they rarely coalesce into an integral historical defense for the Church's picture of Jesus. Instead, they keep pointing, through a certain general skepticism about historical research altogether, to other apologetic concerns. Near the beginning of his long work *Contra Celsum* Origen states outright that "the endeavor to show, with regard to almost any history, however true, that it actually occurred, and to produce an intelligent conception regarding it, is one of the most difficult undertakings that can be attempted, and is in some instances an impossibility" (I:42, trans. from the *Ante-Nicene Fathers* edition, Hendrickson Publishing., 1994). With this dismissal Origen was one of the very few Christians who even bothered to acknowledge queries like Celsus's on their own ground.

On the whole, early Christians, Origen among them, were amazingly insouciant to the historical doubts or concerns about Jesus that critical study might resolve. This is surprising. This insouciance, it appears, was due in large part to another approach, which they saw as far more persuasive and, in the end, coherent with the truth they were attempting to commend to an unbelieving world. A survey of the extant apologetical works of the Early Church supports the gross generalization that Christian thinkers defended their faith in Jesus on two grounds: the consistent moral conversion and moral superiority of Christians compared with non-Christians, and the compelling witness of the Old Testament prophecies to the general history of which these Christians saw themselves a part. Particularly odd is that in many early apologies, such as those of Athenagoras, Aristides, or Theophilus, Jesus as an historical person is not mentioned at all.

Regarding the issue of Christian morals, it is perhaps logical that the apologists stressed Christian moral integrity, since, in many cases, their defenses of Christianity were written in response to persecution and to the specific charges of social corruption made against Christian manners. But this turns out to be only an occasional cause for the emphasis on morals. More crucial to the moral emphasis was the common sense of early Christian apologists that a certain realm of life was involved in the Christian gospel that needed to be both acknowledged and entered into as a condition for apprehending truths pertaining to God—and by extension, to God's Son, the Word himself. This was the realm, in scriptural terms, of holiness. It embraced the goal of the Christian life as well as provided the terms by which the origins and explicators of that life could be grasped. To know God, one must be in some measure like God; to live with God, one must reflect God's own nature, as the apologist Theophilus stressed so clearly at the start of his work *To Autolycus*.

Much of the Early Church's doctrine of salvation was distinctly oriented to the issue of moral conversion. The more elaborate theologies of the incarnation, given early by Clement of Alexandria and later by Athanasius, stress the way in which the coming of the word in the flesh of Jesus took place precisely in order to transform human beings into vessels of righteousness and holiness, whose image conforms to that of God himself. In their apologetical mode, Christians simply took this central understanding of salvation and turned it to the purposes of persuasive argument. "The pious Christian alone is rich and wise, and of noble birth, and thus we must call and believe him to be God's image and also His likeness, having become righteous and holy and wise by Jesus Christ and so far already like God," writes Clement in his *Exhortation to the Heathen* (*Ante-Nicene Fathers* edition of his works, p. 206). The critical test for the argument lay in the manner through which Christians exhibited the holiness they claimed was gained for them by God's word come in Jesus.

Here is where the apologists aimed their heaviest artillery: Christians, they asserted, are demonstrably better, holier, more righteous, and more loving people than non-Christians. It is an argument that few historically informed twentieth-century persons would today wish to make with much conviction. (This argument is still negatively affirmed, however, by those who view the decline of American economics and moral culture as a result of its slide into de-Christianization.) In any case, the argument for Christian holiness is certainly pressed with an astonishing consistency, vigor, and prominence by the early expositors of the faith, from Justin to Tertullian and beyond. "Look at us," they insist, "to understand our religion, observe our sexual abstinence or marital fidelity; note our generosity to strangers; mark our treatment of those who persecute us; attend to our use of money or the way we treat women and slaves, or deal with issues of violence and injustice, poverty and want."

To our post-Reformation ears, this might all seem inappropriately moralistic. But even Augustine, the anti-Pelagian virtuoso, adopted the same line as his predecessors when speaking of the window through which the world can see the illumining clarity of Christ Jesus. Indeed, it is the historical connection they draw between enacted holiness and Christ that is fundamental to distinguishing the early Christian apologists from insistent moralizers. I emphasize "historical" because history and the Jesus of history was crucial to their persuasive presentation of the Christian faith, but in a way that, for very particular reasons, was not available to the enterprise of historical-critical reflection. This brings us to the second common feature of early Christian arguments for the lordship of Jesus the Christ: the fulfillment of scriptural prophecy.

When people like Justin, Tertullian, or Origen called upon pagans to look at the witness of Christian holiness, they took pains to derive that witness from the actual teachings of Jesus, culled from the Gospels. If Christians welcomed the stranger, it was because their Master had taught that one is "to give to whoever asks"; if they were obedient and peaceful, it was because the Teacher whom they followed had spoken of turning the other cheek, of loving enemies, and of being servants; if they accepted death rather than deny their Master, it was because he had showed them the life of the Spirit, of the resurrection, and of the heavenly treasure that the cross could attain.

These teachings of Jesus were often mentioned without reference to the details of Jesus' own life. But they were described as much more than philosophical principles for virtue, for their force was commended in terms of the coherence between actual teachings by a person and the actual lives of his followers. The issue was historical consistency. This was further underlined by the apologists when they attempted to link these teachings of Christ and their fulfillment in the lives of his followers with the lives and teachings of the scriptural prophets who lived long before Jesus and his Church.

The way these early defenders of the Christian faith relied upon rehearsals of the Old Testament prophets as they addressed non-Jews must mystify us. Why would anyone who did not read, let alone believe, the Jewish Scriptures care about what Moses or Isaiah said? And why would anyone be convinced by Christians claiming that certain elements of these prophecies were historically fulfilled through Jesus? This kind of modern question is pertinent because when, in the seventeenth century, the orthodox defense of the lordship and divinity of Christ Jesus took up with a vengeance the argument of the fulfillment of prophecy, the argument increasingly crumbled in the face of historical-criticism, to the point that it is rarely heard today, even in quite conservative circles, and is openly dismissed by most liberal historical critics.

But for the early Christians the compelling character of fulfilled prophecies lay not in the way discrete predictions came to pass. Rather, prophecies were taken as a whole, often without order, to demonstrate the way an entire range of historical realities hung together. The prophets claimed that God's holiness had a certain form, their own lives reflected this form, Jesus' teachings were consistent with this, and Christians, in contrast with pagans and Jews, were in historical conformance with all of this. The early Christian stress upon the fulfillment of prophecy lay in its demonstration of what we can call the historical coherence of the practiced faith of the Christian religion. This demonstration flowered in the great works of historical synthesis by Eusebius, Augustine, and Orosius, who attempted to discern in the events of time, especially in the Roman world, a broad amelioration of corporate sanctity, even in the midst of social disorder (and despite the sorry spectacle of fourth-century Christian divisions). The world and historical experience itself fit, they insisted, with what Christians believe and with the writings they engage at the center of their common life.

Two things should be noted here. The first is the shape of the argument itself: If Isaiah's prediction of a Messiah or king whose rule is given in overwhelming justice is indeed fulfilled, this is so because its confirmation is given in the contemporaneously demonstrable life of the Christian community. The second thing is that this demonstration is grounds for apprehending the content or the significance of the asserted religious truths themselves: who God is and how the prophets actually relate to God's power and Spirit, and who the man Jesus is and why he is called the Christ and our Lord. All of this is exposed not in the confirmation given by the Church's life, but in the taking on of that life—in entering it. That is, in the terms of Theophilus or Clement, entering the realm where the purification of the heart through the instruction of Scriptures, the guiding form of Jesus, and the grace of God's governing Spirit open one's eyes to the glory of his nature and presence.

The early Church's approach to historical reality, then, can be described in this way: the fact of the Church's sanctity, explicated by the Scriptures that point to or describe Christ Jesus, demonstrates the ordering providence of God. And faith in that ordering providence founded the compelling reliability of the scriptural history. Church, Scripture, history: they were at one with each other; they existed in a unity. So if the details of the historical Jesus' life were rarely examined by the apologists, it is because their very existence could not be noted apart from this assumption of the world's providential ordering by God. They belonged to that ordering. The critical testing of historical details was simply unnecessary once they were understood as part of God's providential ordering of history and Scripture as a unit; God, after all, took care of and had already taken care of the details.

What can be noted is the way in which the Church, in her historical coherence with the affirmations of prophecy, made such an ordering plausible, even compelling. As Origen wrote,

It is because Christ was the power of God and wisdom of the Father, announced beforehand by the prophets, that He accomplished and still accomplishes such results, converting not only the wise but the most irrational of men, devoted to their passions, from dissolution to temperance, from injustice to justice, from timidity to courage, such that none have withstood the progress of his teaching—kings and rulers, and the Roman senate and governors in all places, and the common people. (*Contra Celsum*, II:79, trans. in op. cit.)

In contrast, it is possible to move directly to the modern era. That is a big jump, but we can skip the intervening millennium in large measure because the apologetic outlook of the Early Church remained stable though much constricted during this time. We can note, however, that in moments of revival, evangelistic preaching—among the Canons Regular of the twelveth century, and the Franciscans and Dominicans of the thirteenth century, and even the Wycliffites of the fourteenth century—remained tied to the primordial theme of historical coherence, wherein Christ Jesus was to be discovered in the assumption of an existence, in his entry into the world, of a corporate body temporally conformed to the holiness of God described in the Scriptures. There no doubt were scoffers, but the history of Jesus was never called into question. It never became a matter of concern because the premise of a unitary coherence between the Church, history, and Scripture—within which Jesus' life and form assumed a providential force—was still plausible.

A radical change of perspective, however, did indeed take place in the sixteenth century. And by the early seventeenth century, the significance of the Christian faith began to be explicated in a new fashion. The difference between the seventeenth century and this long period before it lay in a novel realization: the historical coherence between Scripture and the Church, which formed the access to an apprehension of Jesus Christ, had become fractured. Whatever the troubles of the Church in the past, the sixteenth-century division of the Western Church, with its resultant religious hostilities and outright warfare that lasted well into the seventeenth century, proved an absolutely devastating contradiction to the prevailing apologetic reliance on communal holiness wrought within the sphere of God's historical providence. The permanent disintegration of the Christian community into antagonistic and competing groups wholly subverted the mutual relation of both sides of the affirmation—scriptural providence and ecclesial virtue.

This is a well-worn observation that has been reasserted in our own day by prominent intellectual historians such as Richard Popkin and Stephen

Toulmin. But the practical theological consequences of the sixteenth-century Church's loss of scriptural and historical credibility, with which we continue to live, have still been underestimated. Protestant apologists adjusted to the new situation by cutting loose scriptural authority from ecclesial virtue; Catholics, on the other hand, tidied up the integrity of providence by simply excising Protestants from the realm of "church" itself. The ripples of these adjustments have magnified over the centuries and have determined many of our present ways of tackling theological matters. Most importantly, a conviction was lost in the process—the conviction that the Christian community's historical experience, because of its conformity to the scriptural narrative and claims, provided the window of access to a clear knowledge of Christ Jesus. The devotional legacy of this evolution, with its radical individualism and loss of communal humility, still haunts us.

The apologetic legacy was even more disruptive. For with the deep skepticism set loose about the historical coherence of Scripture and Church, other avenues were sought after that might demonstrate the attainability of virtue, and the kind of sanctified amelioration of existence that the Early Church had used as its demonstrable access to the person of Jesus. Indeed, by the seventeenth century history itself, with its newly recognized embedded divisions and conflicts intractable to even the Christian Church, needed to be bypassed altogether if salvation was to be properly described and thereby sought after. The rise of historical criticism, at least in the realm of scriptural study, represents just such an attempt to bypass the historical experience of the Church in its relation to scriptural prophecy. It is an effort to get back at the "origins": the origins of Jesus, the origins of his teaching, the origins of his intentions. If Jesus could be described independently of the ecclesial contradictions that had asserted themselves in the sixteenth and seventeenth centuries, independently of what Catholics, Calvinists, Anglicans, Quakers, or Baptists said, then perhaps the still vaguely apprehended salvation he promised might yet be salvaged.

The fact that this salvation now came to be almost exclusively defined in moral terms by the self-consciously modern apologists is not surprising, for it was this moral aspect that ecclesial experience had contradicted. And it was this aspect that seemed so patently demanded by the times, in the face of religious quarrels that had subordinated its importance. Already in the mid-sixteenth century, Christian proponents of religious tolerance, like Sebastien Castellio, found themselves drawn to a rationalistic approach for the reading of Scripture—an approach that tried to strip it of any historically providential power it might once have had—in favor of its distilled moral teachings. By the mid-seventeenth century, the lapsed Jewish philosopher Baruch Spinoza detailed in his *Treatise on Religion and Politics* a kind of primitive manifesto for the historical-critical study of the Bible. Here he called for the writing of a "history of the Scripture," in the same way one might "study Nature," that would identify all the historically contingent and conditioned elements of the biblical texts—their time, place, and context of origin, their authorial idiosyncrasies and projections, their ethnic and socially specific perversions etc, and so forth—and then relegate all of these elements from positions of normative religious authority. Having done this, Spinoza asserted, one would be able to affirm the basic and consistent moral principles that ran through the Bible as a whole (Jesus included), the principles that all people could reasonably accept and follow. This historical approach to the Bible, Spinoza insisted, was absolutely necessary if people were to be freed from the violence brought on by those who, under the "mask of Godly zeal," used the Scriptures to advance their own interests, pressing for "discord and implacable hatred" and attempting to "compel all others to be of their own opinion" (New York: Dover Publications, Inc., 1951, chap. 7).

Only a few decades later the English philosopher John Locke, from a more explicitly Christian vantage point, attempted to do the same thing. He searched in the Scriptures for a universal access to a moral life that might somehow bypass the real antagonisms and particularities of the now warring factions of disintegrated Christianity, particularly obvious in seventeenth-century England. Although Locke was not a historian, he felt that an apprehension of the "real" Jesus of the Scriptures, discerned on his own independent terms, would yield a doctrine wholly conformable to universal human reason, and hence immune to the sectarian strife to which many of his own writings are responses. Many of Locke's followers soon realized that this "real" Jesus of a universal morality of reason was not quite the same as the Jesus of traditional Christianity. With sharpening critical tools, they went about the job of constructing a nonsectarian religion of virtue that could be culled from the Bible, even while the religious particularities of Scripture were rendered obsolete, or time-limited—and therefore discardable—by their efforts at historical analysis.

With an oddly constricted perspicacity, eighteenth-century critical historians, such as Edward Gibbon (*Decline and Fall*, chap. 15), were able to grasp the apologetic force of early Christian holiness, but they were incapable of seeing how such holiness was tied, at least from the Christian perspective, to firm providential and scriptural moorings. (Gibbon, for instance, roundly denigrated early Christian apologists precisely for their reliance on scriptural prophecy, a method he deemed useless.) It was this truncated eighteenth-century vision of Christian origins that led directly to someone like Nietzsche's contempt for Christianity's supposed "moralizing weakness"; indeed, it still informs, if in a less hostile fashion, much contemporary sociological analysis of Christian origins, such as the recent work by Rodney Stark.

One way to characterize the whole historical-critical enterprise as it relates to the Bible in the modern era and continues in our day is to see it as the embodiment of the motive behind a popular bumper sticker that reads, "Jesus, save us from your followers." Who cannot fail to have at least some sympathy with such a hope? Alas, the hope itself is illogical, and its pursuit destructive of its own religious object. For without his followers, it makes no sense to speak of a Jesus who saves. Christ Jesus remains faithful while we are faithless, as Scripture claims (2 Tim. 2:13); but in that case Christ Jesus also remains unknown. Stripped of a church whose life in history conforms to the object of its worship, this Jesus becomes wrapped in obscurities and hidden by arbitrary claims of the moment.

It took decades of struggle within the divided Church before religious tolerance and denominational pluralism became recognized by Locke and others as the logical outcome of nascent historical-criticism's universal morality. And who is not, again, at least a little grateful for the social benefits of that recognition? But even before this process became apparent, John Donne was able to note, if ruefully, the apologetic harvest necessarily reaped by entrenched, accepted, and socially protected Christian division. The product of a family and personal life torn by the Catholic-Protestant rift, Donne wrote the following in one of his *Essays in Divinity*:

> When once the Church is "reduced to unity and agreement," "then, discharged of disputations and misapprehensions and this defensive warr, [she] might contemplate Christ clearly and uniformely. For now he appears to her, as in Cant. 2.9, *He standeth behind a wall, looking forth of the window, shewing himself through the grate.* But then, when all [shall have] one appetite, and one food, one nostrill and one purfume, the Church [will have] obtained that which she had asked. . . [to be] a *savor of life unto life* [that] might allure and draw those to us,

whom our dissention, more then their own stubborness withold from us." (Oxford Unity Press, 1952, p. 52)

This Christ Jesus, whom we confess to believe in as Lord yet now quarrel, recriminate, and divide communion over, is but glimpsed in part, says Donne, as through a distant window grating. It is interesting that Donne makes this remark in the midst of a discussion on the diversity of the scriptural witness, its variations, seeming contradictions, and messiness of reference—all of which would later become the grist for historical criticism and its orthodox opponents (like the indefatigable Nathaniel Lardner who, in the eighteenth century, produced fourteen volumes attempting to iron out the supposed historical discrepancies within the Gospels). But such labors proved fruitless. We cannot see Jesus clearly within this text. The Scriptures strain to give us access to his form, Donne implies, because the Church herself does not coherently embody the Scriptures' providential unity in her own life.

The problem facing the divided Christian churches of our modern era, a problem that both orthodox and less orthodox critical historians cannot hope to resolve, seems to be this: As long as Jesus cannot be affirmed coherently to be the Lord of our history as a Church, he inevitably, no matter what we doctrinally or devotionally claim on our respective ecclesial turfs, is reduced to being a mere subject contained by the unordered history of the past, glimpsed at through the literary fragments of a collection of documents we call the Bible. Historical criticism is a gross reflection of this impasse.

We cannot go back, as John Keble, among others of the Oxford movement, had hoped, simply recovering a patristic view of providence, or of typology and Scripture, or of asceticism, thereby saying of Jesus Christ, "*Ecce homo,* behold the man!" (cf. his essay, "On the Mysticism of the Fathers"). Our emphasis upon early Christian apologetics is not designed to suggest this, nor is our calling to construct or reconstruct some picture of Jesus that will compel and convert or prove our own faithfulness in the face of the apostate. There are plenty of pictures from the last two thousand years that are more than adequate to the demands of God's truth. Still, we must face the sorry fact that we have built a wall around them, through the defenses we have erected around our own Christian communities, one from another, from which we have sallied forth only in hostile pride. The coherence that our history as a Christian community ought to provide—the witness to the Lordship of Christ that holds together Scripture, time, and Christian faith—has been lost, and the commodified culture of Christianity in America is perhaps the nadir of such privation.

By contrast, our confession that "we believe in one Lord, Jesus Christ" will be explicated, and the Scriptures that fulfill that explication will be opened when we are willing to submit our churches to their historical and temporal reshaping into a unified posture of reception from God's ordering hand. That is the note on which this essay might justly stand aside in favor of more constructive critical efforts: theological articulation must be yoked to the mission of ecclesial reconciliation if it is to have any apologetic force at all. Our confession of faith in the one Lord Jesus Christ is not simply a declaration of conviction; it is a profound challenge to any single denomination, and to the larger fractured Church of which we are a part. Our continued confession ought to be properly heard today, less as a proclamation than as a plea crying out: Let us stop the hemorrhaging that our quarrels, our moral dissipation, our self-righteousness, our greed and pride have continued to foster, and that we threaten to display to the world anew with each succeeding step we take. Instead, let us do the work of rebuilding, once again from the ground up, a temple indwelt by the Holy Spirit.

This is not a challenge simply to stir up ecumenical dialogues, or to "just get along," as some church leaders impatiently urge. It is a challenge to recognize and respond to the enforced incapacity of ecclesial witness in our day. The goal, however, is elusive. As institutional churches, as formal Christian communities, we now stand in the same condition as did the first Christians after the resurrection. We have no articulated theology, no proven structures of authority, no experienced framework for the reading of Scripture that is common to us as a church. Is this an opportunity? Certainly it is. But we have been reduced, not raised, to this opportunity through the judgment of God's history. We will not receive from this condition God's grace and power in Christ Jesus, given for life, if we do not first let go of the political and material structures of our institutions, which we continue to use for our self-justification. We then must hold all things in common, as did that young Jerusalem of Christ, pray together, and search the Scriptures anew, in the humble posture of the chastised and not of the holy few.

Each week in every congregation, each month in some church meeting of one kind or another, in one diocese, denomination, or another, there will be a point when all the gathered will proclaim, "We believe in one Lord Jesus Christ." At that point the Lord himself, master of mercy and the forgiver of sins, will offer us yet another chance.

The Only Son of God

K. E. Greene-McCreight   *"the Son of God"*

The confession of Jesus to be "God's only Son, our Lord" is not placed second in the creed, instead of first, because it lacks importance or prominence. In this case, second is not secondary, but rather primary. Indeed, it would not be an overstatement to say that all of Christian confession, from the doctrine of creation to the last things, coheres with the confession of Jesus as the Christ, the Son of the Living God. It is on the basis of the second article that we are able to confess the first and third articles of the creed. Jesus says that "No one knows the Son except the Father, and no one knows the Father except the Son and anyone to whom the Son chooses to reveal him" (Matt. 11:27, Luke 10:22). God the Father is, after all, Father of "His only Son our Lord," and only in Jesus do we know God as Father. So Jesus taught us to pray saying, "Our Father . . ." (Matt. 6:9): our, not his, my, or Great Father God in general. He taught us to pray this way because of his relationship to the God of Israel, a relationship that we secondarily have with the same God through him.

Here is the rub of our confession, the pea under the stack of mattresses, if you will: We proclaim a first-century carpenter named Jesus, from the backwater village of Nazareth, to be the Son of God, the Messiah of Israel, the fulfillment of God's promises to Abraham. This marks the "scandal of particularity," the stone of stumbling on which many have fallen, from the first century right on through to our day. Consider this remark of Celsus, an early pagan detractor of the gospel, whose words are preserved for us in the writings of Origen:

> If these people [Christians] worshipped no other God but one, perhaps they would have a valid argument against the others. But in fact they worship to an extravagant degree this man who appeared recently, and yet think it is not inconsistent with monotheism if they also worship this servant (*Contra Celsum* 8.12, trans. from the *Ante-Nicene Fathers* edition).

Ever since the gospel was first proclaimed, some have found the confession of Jesus to be the Son of God simply too difficult to swallow, and have therefore tried one way or another to separate Jesus from the divine life. This is done by insisting that he is truly man but not truly God, or that he is truly God but not truly man, or by claiming that the Son of God is the divine presence within the disposable container of the historical Jesus. Doing this, however, means setting aside the wisdom of the great cloud of witnesses since Chalcedon, the council at which it was stated that Jesus is fully human *and* fully divine. How do we, in our time, stand in comparison with those at Chalcedon? We would do best to remember two things: (1) how the confession of Jesus as the Son of God assumes the proper unity of the container and the contained, Jesus and the divine life, and (2) how this proper unity is linked to Scripture's portrayal of Jesus' relationship to time, namely to the creation, our own time, and the end of time.

Of course, we know that the gospel's scandal of particularity is not a new problem. It takes Jesus' self-manifestation to break through our resistance. For us to be able to see and confess Jesus as the Son of God. But Christian confession of Jesus as the Son of God has seen new challenges in our time that those before us never faced—challenges that we in our turn must rise to meet. As many of us are painfully aware, the confession of Jesus as "God's only Son, our Lord" has, over the course of the previous two decades, received new mud slung in its direction. The problem of today is not deemed to be the divinity of Jesus, his relation to the Father, or even Jesus' humanity, but it is his very maleness. The complaint goes something like this: The maleness of Jesus "leaks" into the Godhead like a contagion, rendering our understanding of God unclean and, therefore, also our understanding of our own maleness or femaleness. Mary Daly's charge that "If God is male, then Male is God"[1] is accepted in most seminaries as self-evidently true. Now, almost a quarter of a century later, as the result of tacit acceptance of this charge across the denominational spectrum of American Christianity, we have seen numerous revisions of prayer books and hymnals, new translations and paraphrases of the Scriptures, and even reworkings of key doctrines and the Church's very sacraments. This is done with the intent to plug up the leaking masculinity of Jesus and to prevent it from infecting the Godhead, thus keeping the perception of God's masculinity of God from deifying the human male.

The feminist revisions regarding Jesus are in good faith, for the motivating factor is to make him more acceptable and more understandable to the modern American. Many feminists of the Christian faith have made noble attempts to rescue the gospel from the radical feminist charge of Christianity's supposedly "irredeemably patriarchal" nature. Like Bultmann, these feminists intend to remove the unnecessary scandals that would cause people to stumble over Jesus if they remained true to the scandal, which cannot be avoided. They are, in my judgment, about as successful as Bultmann was in this task: wildly popular among theologians, but failing despite their best efforts. One thing that has to be said for feminist theologians, which was also true for Bultmann, is that they are trying their best to apologize, a task with which we can, at the very least, be sympathetic. So the not-so-radical feminists, those still within the Church, attempt to show how the Church has distorted the identity of Jesus over the centuries. They then try to reclaim the Christ that is untainted by the patriarchal, hierarchical theology of the Church. The effect of the project, however, is the separation of the contents from the container, or, in contemporary parlance, the separation of the Jesus of history from the Christ of faith.

Because an example, more than an explanation, speaks volumes, I will illustrate this claim with the work of Patricia Wilson-Kastner, who was one of our priests and a member of the College of Preachers. She wrote:

> For our purposes the vexing issue is how Christianity—in four or five centuries—moved from an egalitarian Jesus of the Gospels who accepted women as human beings on par with men, to an exclusivistic Christ, one who was portrayed by the Church with increasing frequency as a figure of male excellence.[2]

In order to recover the "inclusivistic Christ," as she called him, Wilson-Kastner made use (usually implicitly) of the conceptual dichotomy between the Jesus of history and the Christ of faith. This dichotomy itself is nothing new. I do not intend to fault feminist theologians for using a category with long-standing precedence in modern theology. I do question, however, the theological legitimacy of that precedence itself. But this dichotomy is the root of the problem with many feminist Christologies, and it is usually the unacknowledged bond of intellectual and spiritual unity between many feminist theologians and scholars of the historical Jesus.

The distinction between the Jesus of history and the Christ of faith was developed in eighteenth- and nineteenth-century theology and biblical criticism, beginning with Reimarus's attack on the Gospels as a "tissue of lies," which he claimed the Church had woven to cover up what he saw to be a failed religious leader. Reimarus is an exceptionally contemporary figure. Born in 1694, the same year as Voltaire, his writings were not published until the second half of the eighteenth century, after his death. Yet much of what the Jesus Seminar is doing is based on the presuppositions of Reimarus. Reimarus assumed, as many still do, that there is a distinction between the Jesus of history and the Christ of faith, and that there is a "Jesus as he really was," who can be unearthed from the sedimentary layers of Christian confession that were imposed on him in the New Testament record. The dichotomy itself is philosophically and historically nonsensical, not to mention theologically impossible, when examined closely, but exploring this is not my purpose.

The use of the dichotomy between the Jesus of history and the Christ of faith appears in much of feminist Christology, whether openly acknowledged or not, as a conceptual crowbar to separate the contents (Christ) from the container (Jesus). Although feminist Christologies and the work of the Jesus Seminar are materially different, the logic with which they operate is formally quite similar. Feminist Christologies tend to want to reduce Jesus' maleness in theological significance, and, in order to do so, focus on the Christ of faith, who is more interesting to the feminist project. The man Jesus of Nazareth thus becomes the "Box One," which contains the mystery prize of the Christ of faith, and a new package is sought that will supposedly be more appropriate to what is found inside. Now, in much historical Jesus research, such as exemplified in the Jesus Seminar, the focus is on what presumably can be determined about the container, and this is used to reconfigure the contents of the box. Both projects, however, are under the faulty assumption that Jesus of Nazareth can somehow be isolated or separated from the Christ: the two figures cannot be separated without ignoring the witness of the New Testament.

As Martin Kähler pointed out over a century ago, the Gospels, our source for understanding who Jesus was, are such that it is impossible to split the Jesus of Nazareth from the Christ. There is no Christ figure apart from Jesus, as he is depicted in the Gospels. It is a logical impossibility and a conceptual error to claim that we can strip away the Church's confessional accretions from the historical nuggets in the Gospels and come up with a "Jesus as he actually was." For example, it is often assumed by modern scholarship that the resurrection narratives depict Jesus as the Church wanted him to be, and that this Jesus-as-the-Church-wanted-him-to-be is the Christ of faith. This figure, so it is assumed, has relatively little correspondence with who Jesus really was. However, a casual reading of the resurrection appearance narratives confirms that their intention is to show that Jesus as he was before that fateful Friday is still the same figure on the following Sunday, even with the obvious differences entailed in his passing "through death and out the other side," to use a phrase borrowed from Tom Wright. The purpose of the narratives about Jesus' resurrection appearances is not to prove to us that Jesus' dead body was resuscitated, nor that his ghost appeared to the disciples, nor that Jesus metamorphosed into the Christ, like a worm emerges as a butterfly after entering the cocoon. The point of the New Testament resurrection-appearance narratives is to show that the Jesus whom the disciples encountered after his burial is the very same Jesus with whom they had lived, traveled, and ate and drank, the very same Jesus whose death they had witnessed, and the very same Jesus whom they now more fully understood to be the Messiah of Israel and the Son of the living God. The Jesus of history, if by this phrase we mean the earthly Jesus, *is* the Christ of faith. There is no separating one from the other.

However, when scholars claim that such a separation is indeed possible, the result is usually a Jesus of history who looks very much like his reconstructors. Albert Schweitzer noted this almost one hundred years ago in his *The Quest for the Historical Jesus*. This is just as true now as it was during the "Old Quest," when we were offered portrait after portrait of a blond-haired, blue-eyed Aryan Jesus. Now late twentieth-century American academicians portray Jesus as a revolutionary antiestablishment sophist, and, using similar logic, feminist scholars paint Jesus to be a female Christ figure. We should not be surprised. However, we should ask ourselves: Will we allow Jesus to be Jesus as he is presented by those who knew him best, the gospel writers, or do we insist on remaking him after our own image and likeness?

Jesus of Nazareth, as the gospel writers depict him, was a man, a male Jew. This is problematic in light of Rosemary Radford Ruether's now classic question, "Can a male savior save women?" and the often negative answer: No, a male savior cannot save women. Those with this response will either reject Christianity entirely, as have Daphne Hampson and Mary Daly, or attempt to separate the mysterious contents of the Christ from the container of the male Jesus. To illustrate this, I turn again to Patricia Wilson-Kastner:

> To identify Jesus with maleness (or Jewishness, or living in the first
> century, and so forth) is to miss the point of Jesus' significance and
> mission . . . The Christ whom we are considering is, after all, the living
> Christ, not simply a Palestinian rabbi of the first century. This Christ
> is the Incarnation of the eternal Word of God. . . .[3]

Similarly, another of our theological educators, Ellen Wondra, who has taught at Bexley Hall, says in the same vein:

> Jesus' being male has revelatory importance only because of the
> meaning of maleness in patriarchal history and culture. The fact that
> Jesus' relations with others were self-giving, inclusive, reciprocal or
> mutual, cooperative and just stands against the patterns and
> conventions of patriarchy, which operate to the benefit of men of
> dominant groups and to the detriment of women and other
> marginalized persons.[4]

One could continue to quote feminist theologians with such thinking, for these two women are by no means unique in this respect.

Answering Ruether's question in the negative, however, denies the reality of classical Christian eschatology. The New Testament understands Jesus' resurrection to be the eschatological event par excellence. His resurrection forms the linchpin between two time zones. According to the New Testament, Jesus is the firstfruits of the general resurrection: in his rising from the dead the end of the ages has dawned. Feminist abandoning of classical Christian eschatology is startling in many ways, for it undermines the basis of any biblically grounded feminism, and thus implicitly permits an antifeminism among those who stand on the authority of Scripture.

Denying classical Christian eschatology, when combined with the modern dichotomy between the Jesus of faith and the Christ of history, lands us in a tragic cul-de-sac. At the risk of being misunderstood, we might even venture the thesis that Jesus' maleness is in some respect salvifically significant. Just as Jesus' Jewishness is soteriologically important, so is his maleness. Of course, in philosophical terms, Jesus' maleness is indeed an "accident," but in terms of the biblical narrative, Jesus had to be a man, indeed, a male Jew. Jesus was the Son of God and the Son of Mary, fully divine and fully human. We are born with the physical and hormonal makeup that marks us as either male or female. Few feminist theologians actually want to deny Jesus' maleness. But they do want to deny that his being male is related to his soteriological significance. However, since Jesus was a Jew who fulfilled the promises to Israel and once and for all offered up the perfect sacrifice, he had to be male. If he were not a male, and a Jew— a free Jewish male—how could the baptismal promise of Galatians 3:27–29 have been granted?

> For as many of you as were baptized into Christ have put on Christ. There is neither Jew nor Greek, there is neither slave nor free, there is neither male nor female; for you are all one in Christ Jesus. And if you are Christ's then you are Abraham's offspring, heirs according to the promise.

The three sets of opposition in verse 28, Jew and Greek, slave and free, male and female, correspond to the categories in which Jewish election is cast. God freely bestows his grace on Abraham, a male, and his descendants. The religiously observant male Jew praises God every day for creating him male and not female, Jewish and not Gentile. In the conservative prayer book, though not in the orthodox prayer book, the male Jew also gives thanksgiving to God for making him free and not a slave like his ancestors in Egypt. These are the marks of Jewish election. In Galatians, Paul says that what has happened in Jesus has turned this election on its head: In the new "time zone" inaugurated by Jesus' resurrection there is no distinction in God's electing grace between Jew and Gentile, slave and free, male and female. Christian eschatology therefore undercuts any possibility that Jesus' maleness somehow excludes or bypasses women, that it could somehow uplift the male over the female. Eschatology formally disallows the male lording over the female in the body of Christ.

So returning to Ruether's question, "Can a male savior save women?" the answer is, yes, because Jesus did, but also, to address the concerns of feminist theology, because in him the end of the ages has dawned. The relationship between male and female has taken a radical turn, and the fallen order has become the new creation. In the time zone inaugurated by the resurrection of Jesus, the curse of Genesis 3 has been turned around. Most feminist theologians have not sufficiently dealt with the implications of this. In

Genesis 3:16, God says the following to Eve after the disobedience in the garden: "Your desire shall be for your husband, and he shall rule over you." These words form the *locus classicus* of the biblical view of sexism's origin and shape. The male's rule over the female is one of the many results of Adam and Eve's disobedience to the Creator. Humanity had been created good; "Behold, it was very good!" (Gen. 1:31). But after the first "theological conversation" in the garden, and the consequent disobedience to the will of God, everything was cursed. In Jesus Christ, however, we have been made new creatures: "The old has passed away, behold, the new has come" (2 Corinthians 5:17). It took the death of this male Jewish Messiah, the unblemished Lamb of God, the only begotten Son of God, to accomplish the transition from the old order to the new. This, by the way, is the real reason it makes no sense to block the ordination of women solely on the grounds of gender. To assume that males can represent Christ more easily or fully than females is a theological error, somewhat analogous to the feminist confusion that women cannot be saved by a male savior. It is not a justice issue, but a Christological one and therefore a matter of eschatology. The end of the ages indeed has dawned in him.

This only makes sense to those well-steeped in the biblical narrative, to those well-catechized and formed by the sacraments and worship of the Church. After all, things have not changed much since the Apostle to the Gentiles penned these lines:

> For the word of the cross is foolishness to those who are perishing, but to us who are being saved it is the power of God. . . . For Jews demand signs and Greeks seek wisdom, but we preach Christ crucified, a stumbling block to Jews and foolishness to Gentiles, but to those who are called, both Jews and Greeks, Christ the power of God and the wisdom of God. For the foolishness of God is wiser than humans, and the weakness of God is stronger than humans. (1 Cor. 1:18, 22-25)

These verses may come across as arrogance to those who, for whatever reason, cannot accept the gospel of Jesus Christ. However, if these people were to look at Jesus long enough, to allow themselves to see him for what he is as portrayed in Scripture—the Son of God, the gift that is both the container and the contents—they might not be offended after all. "Why, what hath my Lord done, what makes this rage and spite? He made the lame to run, he gave the blind their sight. Sweet injuries, yet they at these themselves displease and 'gainst him rise" (Samuel Crossman, "My Song Is Love Unknown").

Although Jesus heals the gender struggle that was a result of the Fall, we allow him to be accused of causing our gender grief. We are displeased with the agent of our healing. The human heart is hell-bent on being displeased with Jesus. Ceaseless debates over the historical Jesus and the Christ of faith, and over the pain caused by his maleness, will allow the question our Lord poses to us to be endlessly deferred: "Who do you say that I am?" (Mk. 8:29).

If we allow the charges against Jesus to shape our confession of him as the Son of God, we will need to reweave our entire web of belief. This in and of itself is not objectionable, provided that what we end up saying about Jesus and his relationship to the Father and to the Spirit could be true. However, the Church since the earliest creeds has understood them to speak, as though in a nutshell, of the truth to which Scripture witnesses. To claim that we can have access to the Triune God apart from Scripture and the creed is to claim too much for ourselves before that final day, when we shall see Jesus face to face as he is.

---

[1]Mary Daly, *Beyond God the Father* (Boston: Beacon Press, 1973) 19.

[2]Patricia Wilson-Kastner, *Faith, Feminism, and the Christ* (Philadelphia: Fortress Press, 1983), 71.

[3]Ibid., 90–91.

[4]Ellen K. Wondra, *Humanity Has Been a Holy Thing: Toward a Contemporary Feminist Christology* (Lanham, MD: University Press of America, 1994), 304.

Jesus Christ and the Moral Life

The Rev. Dr. Stephen Carl Holmgren

"Maker of heaven and earth"

O God of unchangeable power and eternal light: Look favorably on your whole Church, that wonderful and sacred mystery; by the effectual working of your providence, carry out in tranquility the plan of salvation; let the whole world see and know that things which were cast down are being raised up, and things which had grown old are being made new, and that all things are being brought to their perfection by him through whom all things were made, your son Jesus Christ our Lord. *Amen.* (The Book of Common Prayer, 1979:291)

A story is told about a visit by the poet Coleridge to a waterfall. At the scene Coleridge encounters two other visitors who are commenting on their reaction to the wonderful sight before them. One of the visitors calls the waterfall "sublime." The other visitor refers to it simply as "pretty." Overhearing their conversation, Coleridge agrees with the first but not the second assessment of the stirring sight. This story and the reaction of two modern writers to it are reported by C.S. Lewis in his book *The Abolition of Man.*[1] Lewis uses the story as a way in which to raise questions about the nature of our response to aspects of the world. What does it mean to call a waterfall "sublime"? Lewis wants us to ask: Do judgments of aesthetic or moral value record actual qualities of the things that we encounter in the world? Or do responses expressed in words like "sublime" and "pretty" merely indicate something about the inner experience of the viewer? Though it is not at first obvious, these questions have a great deal of theological significance.

As Christians who confess all things were made through our Lord Jesus Christ, we may find ourselves prompted to ask whether all things were made with moral value. In other words, in the Christian view of the world, is moral value to be found *in the things* that have been made, in the objects of our experience? Or, shall we say that moral value is something that is more properly sought and encountered in *the subjects* of moral experience, in our thoughts and feelings as they are shaped by our encounter with Jesus? These questions take us to the heart of our Christology and of our doctrine of redemption, and they lead us to consider the significance of Jesus for the moral life.

Where and how does Jesus make a difference in our world and in our ethics? There are at least two general ways of answering this question, which unfortunately have become separated in recent ethics and moral theology. We can say that Jesus makes a difference in our ethics by the way his resurrection transforms our hearts and minds, and thus by the way in which he transforms the subjective wellsprings of our moral action. We can also say that Jesus makes a difference in our ethics by the way in which his resurrection transforms the world of our moral action, both in the way that our action is shaped and in the way the world in which we act is simultaneously transformed. These two answers, one focusing on the inward transforming power of Jesus upon human subjectivity and the other Jesus' transformation of the world of objects and action, have tended to become separated to the diminishment of the outward, or objective, reference point for ethics. As a result, one will find in recent works of ethics and moral theology a greater stress on the inward, or subjective, aspects of Christian ethical experience. It is my goal here to argue for the inseparability of the inward and outward ethical aspect, to demonstrate their interconnection in Jesus Christ, through whom *all things* were made.

A most interesting, if not also unexpected, example of an emphasis upon the subjective aspects of ethics can be found in the later writings of the Polish ethicist Karol Wojtyla, who is better known as John Paul II. Especially in his encyclical, *Veritatis Splendor,* John Paul tends to focus on the inner dynamics of moral subjectivity, that is to say, upon the function of reason and will, upon conscience and reflection, in the shaping of moral action. Oliver O'Donovan, a successor of Kenneth Kirk as the Regius Professor of Moral and Pastoral Theology at Oxford, has drawn attention to this emphasis, which the encyclical shares with many other contemporary writings. He observes: "What is lacking in contemporary trends in moral thought is a sense of moral order in the world."[2] As a result of these trends, moral action is seen as something that "is shaped to the service of the moral agent-mind or agent-will, rather than to the service of the world." In effect, moral action is shaped more in terms of its subject than its object. It comes to lose what O'Donovan calls "its world-determined meaning as action." He questions whether John Paul can "repair this [loss of moral order in the world] with a stress on moral order in the mind."

The source of this lack of a sense of moral order in the world is not hard to trace. At the time of the Reformation and at the beginning of the Enlightenment, two things occurred that together had a discouraging result for claims about moral order in the world. The first of these is the renewal of theology, which was accompanied in the Church by a generous amount of vigorous debate. The fact that men and women were exiled, and that lives were lost, fostered the conclusion that religious differences are ultimately irreconcilable through reasonable discourse, and that religion is best viewed as a private matter, rather than as a part of the public bond between persons in society. The second occurrence is the birth of modern empirical, or natural, science, which was accompanied by a gradual withdrawal of religious claims into the private and personal sphere. If religious claims about truth and the nature of reality were no longer the source of consensus, then some other mechanism for explaining the nature of the world might come into play, especially one which was based not on theoretical speculation, but on empirical observation and the use of reason. No longer would observation of the world yield understanding of its meaning, purpose and moral significance. Instead, what one observed in the objects of experience were factual qualities that could be recorded and compared. Moral value was something that was apprehended in the moral subject, in our own minds and hearts, and not in the physical object. Put very simply, we find here the gradual separation between fact and value, with the result that many of us today quite naturally speak of facts as something that objects possess, and values as something that people have. Not only are values something that are now seen as residing primarily in moral subjects, in our hearts and minds, but we tend to think of values as something *we project onto* things or other persons. An object or an act has a particular moral value because I invest it with this quality. It has value because consciously or unconsciously I choose to look at it in this way. It is no surprise to me if the object looks different to you, for you have your own values, and you see facts differently than I do.

All this represents quite a change from the worldview of persons in the classical world, and in the patristic and medieval church. Up until the time of the Reformation and beyond, we can see a different and earlier approach in the thought of Christian writers, especially in the Catholic tradition of moral thought. Within this tradition in the West, which includes both Anglican and Roman Catholic writers, there has been a general confidence in the existence of a moral order in the structure of the world, as well as in the structures of human subjectivity. This moral order is seen as a legacy of God's hand in Creation, which has endured through the Fall and which undergoes renewal and transformation in God's work of Redemption. Natural law and natural theology are the terms usually associated with this view of moral order, a view that is often associated with the philosophy of Aristotle and the theology of Thomas Aquinas. This approach, however, is certainly not unknown in the writings of Luther, Melanchthon, and Calvin, and these ideas sometimes make an appearance in the works of Protestant writers, in connection with the concept of created order. Richard Hooker is the best-known exponent within Anglicanism of this approach to moral order. Lisa Cahill, a contemporary, Roman Catholic ethicist, characterizes such an approach to moral order in the following way: "Natural law moral thinking, rooted in Aquinas and visible in different ways in sexual teachings, bioethics, just war theory, and the social encyclicals, works from reasonable and critical generalizations on shared human experience. It is confident that moral common ground can be established among people with different cultural and religious traditions."[3] This confidence is based on the theological assumption that these reasonable and critical generalizations reflect an order that is rooted in the structure of creation, and not simply in the hearts and minds of individual believers. We can certainly become focused on the extent to which, either through sin or ignorance, we are capable of ignoring, misperceiving, or disagreeing about the content of this order. We can also discern a pattern of reticence among certain strands of the Protestant tradition about our ability to recognize such an order. Yet, focusing on such differences will likely distract us from the theological confidence shared by so many of our forebears that the Psalmist's utterance, "The heavens declare the glory of the Lord, and the firmament shows forth his handiwork" (Psalm 19:1), is an assertion that has both moral and spiritual significance.

Now there is, of course, a considerable amount of critical thought, particularly in the field of philosophy, that has nurtured the drift away from this viewpoint, which is confident of a given moral order in God's creation, to one that has confidence only in the power of human subjectivity to create moral order. One of the most accessible treatments of this shift in viewpoint is C.S. Lewis's *The Abolition of Man*. The basic issue here is whether or not human subjectivity apprehends the foundations for morality in our experience of reality, in the structure of the objective world. This is a problem in moral philosophy, as well as a central question in Christian moral thought. Not only is there a question of whether or not the foundations for morality are *really there,* in the structure of creation, but there is also the question of whether or not we can reliably apprehend and know those foundations, if they are there. Within the field of moral philosophy there seems to be a return to a greater degree of confidence, at least in the works of some writers, in what might be called an "externalist" approach, an approach that is willing to consider moral order in the world.[4] There is also a growing body of work, both in and about the natural sciences, that is more willing to consider a compatibility between these fields and that of theology.

In any event, my purpose is not to survey moral philosophy or the natural sciences. My goal is to urge us to take more seriously the theological significance of some our central claims. Chief among these is the phrase that is my title, "through him all things were made." My aim is ambitious in that I wish to join O'Donovan and others in helping to reclaim the vast domain of creation, the realm of the objects of attention and experience, as a proper domain for the apprehension and discernment of the moral good. My aim is modest in that I will prescind from identifying precisely and specifically what some of the manifold instances or manifestations of that good are. Because we have found it so hard in today's world to say *how* something is the case, for example, how the moral good is apprehended in creation, we have lost our confidence that it is so, that there is moral order to be found in creation. This is the reductionist problem: of saying that *because* we cannot agree on *what* we are going to have for dinner tonight, we should doubt *that* we are going to have dinner. Yet, the fact that there is moral order to be found in creation—"through him through whom all things were made"—is what I wish to emphasize here. In doing so, I want it to be clear that I am not seeking simply to revive a particular concept of moral order, such as the crudely physicalist stereotypes of natural law, which modern moralists like to use in straw-man arguments. Instead, and more positively, I wish to offer a sketch of what a theological approach to a creation and redemption-based moral order might look like.

My offering is set in the key of C, for *continuity*—continuity between God's mighty act of creation and God's mighty act of redemption; continuity between the record of God's saving activity in the Old Covenant and that of the New; continuity between the realm of nature and that of grace; and continuity between the shape of God's saving activity in the life, death, and resurrection of Jesus Christ and that of our response to it in an ethical life centered on the Eucharist. The voices heard in this small offering are those of the Bible, the prayer book, and the Hymnal. In choosing to use texts from the prayer book and hymnal, I want it be clear that I am not subscribing to a popular form of positivism. This is the positivism of assuming that a liturgical text is true simply because the General Convention or General Synod has said so. If any text is true, it is true because it conforms to and complements truth as it is encountered in the special revelation of Scripture, *and* in the general revelation we encounter in creation.

As we embark, we can observe in many works of twentieth-century moral theology a trend parallel to that already mentioned. This is the trend away from reference to moral order in the structure of creation and toward moral order in the structure of human subjectivity. It may be seen in yet another unexpected example, in the works of Kenneth Kirk, which are usually credited with spurring a renaissance in contemporary Anglican moral theology. Kirk's writings are generally no longer used as a starting point for teaching Christian ethics or moral theology in Anglican or Episcopal seminaries. This is because his work has gained the reputation of being based upon a rigid, or static, metaphysical view of reality. If this were true, his approach would provide an inadequate foundation for morality in a church that has become more sensitive to the vagaries of human experience and to the evolution of human historical consciousness. Yet all this assumes that this reading of Kirk is correct, and that there is good reason to doubt it. Here and there a few readers are once again picking up his books and are beginning to recognize that Kirk had anything but a rigid or static view of the world.[5]

A good way to gain a quick indication of where Kirk or any ethicist believes we are to apprehend moral order is to look at the table of contents of his or her work. Is creation or human subjectivity the primary reference point? Does the author give equal attention to the objects and the subjects of moral experience and action? This can be done quite often with writers who work within the Catholic tradition by examining their treatment of the topics that correspond to what has traditionally been called natural law and conscience. Because the general shift in contemporary thought toward discerning moral value within human subjectivity, it has become characteristic of recent works to treat conscience, or human moral subjectivity, first. Many of these authors then approach the topic of moral order in the world—or natural law—as a feature that is apprehended through the structures of human subjectivity. In these works, human subjectivity is then often credited with giving additional shape to natural moral order. In this respect, Kenneth Kirk's basic text, *Some Principles of Moral Theology,* surprisingly has much in common not only with *Veritatis Splendor* but also with such contemporary texts as Charles Curran's *Directions in Fundamental Moral Theology* and Richard Gula's *Reason Informed by Faith*—texts that may fairly be described as forward-looking in Catholic moral theology.[6]

This shift toward giving primary attention to conscience in ethics, to the realm of human moral subjectivity, and to the complexity of human perception and knowing is a legacy of the Enlightenment. The shift is directly related to the gradual acceptance of the separation between fact and value. Ethics and the discernment of value, because they are seen as involving reason, tend to become identified with moral subjectivity. By contrast, the world in which we act tends to be relegated to the realm of science and technology in terms of study and application. The acceptance of such a separation between ideas that belong together is reflected in other examples of the same problem; I suspect that all of these separations are directly related. We now tend to separate the Jesus of history, the Jesus who grew up in Nazareth as a builder's son and became a charismatic teacher, from the Christ of faith, the Christ who rose from the dead and helps to shape our experience of resurrection today. We also tend to separate spirituality from ethics, just as we separate salvation history from what we call natural history.

The common consequence of these separations is a worldview through which many of us now look at ourselves and our lives. We have an interior spiritual life which is centered on the risen Christ of faith, who shapes our consciousness, that tends to be compartmentalized. At the same time, but yet disconnected from our spirituality, we have material lives that are involved in the particularities and ethical challenges of the natural world and modern society, a world we believe is far removed from Jesus' first-century world of Palestine. In my view, the consequences for Christian ethics of this "convergence of separations" is fairly disastrous. The problem is that in accepting these separations as normative, we have come to assume the presence of a division at the center of some of the most important aspects of our faith and life. It is no wonder that many of us have turned to spirituality as our Christian preoccupation, especially in the face of confusion and turmoil in the field of ethics, where there seems to be so little agreement about starting points, methods, and content, much less about whether or not it is right to kiss on a first date!

One example of the effect of these separations is the way in which we approach our spirituality, as compared with our ethics. In the sphere of spirituality, many of us appear to be more prepared to accept the notion of an overlapping commonness to the pattern of life our Lord has provided for us. Though we are certainly capable of disagreeing about liturgical texts, we still readily use and remain committed to having common forms of prayer, and we proclaim in our baptismal rite that we have one Lord, one faith, one God and Father of us all. And yet, in the sphere of ethics we hesitate when it comes to the proposal that our Lord has set before us—a similar degree of commonness in the patterns provided for righteousness. For some reason, we can accept and are comfortable with certain generic ways of experiencing the nearness of God in the realm of spirit and prayer. But when it comes to ethical action, we seem to think that our growth in righteousness must be characterized by particularity and uniqueness.

Not only should a pious deference to tradition cause us to hesitate over the separation of the spiritual and the ethical, but so also should a regard for our embodiment; for the embodiment of our Lord; and for his creation, redemption, and eschatological completion of the world of things, persons, and actions. We pray that we might give up ourselves *to walk in holiness and righteousness* all our days. When we allow the spiritual and ethical to drift apart, we diminish the significance of what we say we believe. We do the same when we allow attention to the ethical formation of our hearts, souls, or character to become detached from the moral shape of our lived lives, from our lived acts.

Let us further consider the way in which we view spirituality and the way in which we think of ethics. In spirituality, with regard to the realm of what we call the soul, we seem to find it appropriate to speak of Christ's sovereignty over our hearts as the king of love, or over the formation of our character as the giver of true virtue. An increasing amount of attention is being paid to these themes in recent works of moral theology where the focus is predominately directed to the sphere of moral subjectivity. We should ask if the same thing is true in our approach to bodily lived daily life. In our own ethics or moral theology, do we have a similar regard for Christ's sovereignty over the actual shape of our lived lives and our lived acts? To see if we are in danger of collapsing our ethics into spirituality, we should test whether we have an embodied faith in an increasingly disembodied age. For example, do we approach living in a way that reflects real confidence in Jesus Christ as the source and the completion of the ways in which we use our material goods and possessions—our money, time, sexuality and all of our embodied involvements? With this question I go—as the old saying puts it—from preaching to meddling! I am afraid that, with regard to many of these aspects of daily life, it has become more convenient for us to accept without protest the gradual separation of the Christ of faith from the Jesus of history. In so doing, we accept a separation between the realm of the religious or spiritually formed heart, and the bodily world of natural involvements, as well as and the practical ethics that go with them.

A proper regard for the incarnation of our Lord requires more than this. A proper regard for God's Trinitarian relation to creation requires more, and a proper regard for our sacramental participation in Jesus' ministry requires more than this acceptance of an ungodly separation. The challenge we face can be articulated with the help of some further questions. Can we describe the shape of the redeemed life and redeemed human action as well as we can describe the quality of the redeemed heart and personality? Does attention to the shape of a redeemed creation inform our view of the moral life? Or, do we prefer to rely on the impact of Christ on our experience of moral subjectivity for guidance in living a baptismal life? What is the significance of offering worked bread, formed by human hands, instead of simple kernels of wheat or oats on the altar? Are not the bread and wine powerfully symbolic of bodily involvements and their latent potential to glorify the risen Lord? And are there not identifiable patterns of manifest righteousness or godliness in our bodily involvements, that can bring glory to the Lord who made them, redeemed them, and brings them to fullness in himself?

The words of Aurelius Prudentius, an ancient Christian whose writings still live in our hymnal, provide a compelling focus for us as we consider these questions. In a text that is usually sung during the Christmas season, Prudentius writes about Jesus:

Of the Father's love begotten
ere the worlds began to be
he is Alpha and Omega
he the source, the ending he
of the things that are, that have been
and that future years shall see
evermore, evermore[7]

In these words, translated by John Mason Neale, Prudentius gives voice to the view that all reality has its source *and ending* in the Son. He expresses in poetry what we confess in the creed, that "through him all things were made." Yet Prudentius says *more*, that not only were all things made through him, but that all things have their ending, summation, or fulfillment in him. All things! Not just the realm of prayer and spirituality, not just the realm of faith and confession, not just the realm of angels and grace, but all things in the whole of creation have their beginning and end in him.

The problem for us is that we are too enamored with just one of the ways that we are created in God's image and likeness. Like our God, in a derivative way, we too are creators. We create action. We create acts. We shape them, and we give them meaning. Our capacity for self-initiated action becomes both a source of pride and a source of blindness. We imagine, at least with respect to the sphere of will and action, that we are autonomous, independent, and self-ruled. This prevalent form of self-perception is also a legacy of the modern period; it goes hand in hand with the separations we have already noted between fact and value, between spirituality and ethics. On one hand, we can think of spirituality as something that God does in us in our interior lives. On the other hand, we can think of ethics as tied to the world of action, which is something we create ourselves. Since the latter originates in us, it is in some way disconnected from the former, or at least the connection is indirect. God shapes us. Quite separately from this, or so we imagine, we are shapers of action. However, two things have been forgotten here. First, we have forgotten that our acts also shape us, and that good or bad acts help shape good or bad character. Secondly, we have forgotten that acts and choices are things in themselves that are features of the reality that has its beginning and end in Christ. Acts and choices, in their basic pattern or structure, are also shaped by God and are therefore given moral value by him.

As I have already said, it is not my purpose to instantiate precisely how it is that specific kinds of moral action have their beginning and end in him. That is an important but subsidiary task. My purpose here is simply to urge us to consider believing that, along with the world itself and all the things within it, specific kinds of moral action also have their beginning and end in him. I find myself prompted to consider the possibilities inherent in Paul's words to the Ephesians: "For we are God's handiwork, created in Christ Jesus to devote ourselves to the good deeds for which God has designed us."(Eph. 2:10). The shape of those good deeds to which Paul refers, suggests, owes just as much to the creative handiwork of God in Jesus Christ as we do.

My point is this: I believe that we should take more seriously the significance of the words that many of us pray at least every week, if not every day. For example, many of us pray, "We humbly beseech thee, O heavenly Father, so to assist us with thy grace, that we may continue in that holy fellowship, and do all such good works as thou hast prepared for us to walk in."[8] With these words, we give voice to the idea that God has made and provided particular good works for us, and we ask for strength to pursue them. Clearly, God calls each one of us to serve him in ways that are common to us all and in ways that are particular to the individual. We are all called to praise him, to love him with our whole being, and to serve his creation as a part of the stewardship given to Adam and Eve. We are called to walk in love, as Christ loved us and gave himself for us, an offering and sacrifice to God. By contrast, *I* am called to serve him in a particular way as the ethics professor at Nashotah House, just as you may be called to serve him as an insurance claims adjuster. The point I want to recognize here is that Christian vocation has both common or generic elements to it, as well as the particular.

There is a common overlapping pattern to the way in which we are drawn up into God's purposes in redemption. This pattern mirrors, of course, the fact that there is a common overlapping pattern to God's purposes in creation. Many spheres of human action provide avenues of expression for the divinely provided pattern of human well-being and redemption. Just as we do not save ourselves, but are utterly dependent upon God in Jesus Christ to lift us up into the new life of Christian baptism, so too are we dependent upon God in Jesus Christ to bring us into holiness and righteousness. We may exercise the will to act for the good. But the pattern of action that manifests the good and provides the context for our growth in righteousness is surely among the things that, through him, were made. If Jesus is the Alpha of our daily walk in holiness and righteousness, he is surely also its Omega.

It is inconceivable to me that we should ever consider the moral life as somehow residing outside of the upholding providential hands of God in Jesus Christ. If we are willing to grant the truth of this in principle, why not also in all the specific acts of our daily practice? If we are comfortable saying that, at a general level, "in him we live and move and have our being," should we not also say this with respect to our use of money, time, our bodies, or relationships? So that in all the ways we use these things, we do so in him? It seems odd to me that we should be prepared to answer "yes" to all of these questions, and yet not also imagine that there is a pattern to these choices that we make—some overlapping way in which these good works are present in my life as well as in yours.

Surely, Christian baptismal life presumes this. When we pledge to continue in the Apostles' teaching and fellowship, in the breaking of bread, and in the prayers, we are committing ourselves to activities that represent a common overlapping pattern between us. This pattern is recognizable. Not the least of the examples of this pattern is our way of giving thanks to God in the Eucharist. I believe that the challenge lying before us as a Church, and more particularly before the bishops of the Church, is the articulation of the common overlapping patterns of righteousness that, through our Lord Jesus Christ, were made. Let us take up this challenge, and let us not allow our preoccupation with church discipline to get in the way of our need to inspire moral vision. Let us devote ourselves to setting before the Church a clearer view of is common pattern for living, which fleshes out what resisting evil means, or what repentance and returning to the Lord mean for human action. Let us say what it means to seek and serve Christ in all persons with our bodies, time, money, and energy. And let us seek a clearer notion of what common, created ways our Lord Jesus has provided for us, to respect the dignity of every person. As we seek this clarity, let us not hesitate to believe that, when through him all things were made, a common, articulable patterns of holiness and righteousness was among the things that were made.

---

[1]C.S. Lewis, *The Abolition of Man* (New York: Simon & Schuster [Touchstone], 1996), p. 18.

[2]For this and the following quotations, see *Considering Veritatis Splendor,* edited by John Wilkins (Cleveland: The Pilgrim Press, 1994).

[3]Lisa Sowle Cahill, "Accent on the Masculine," in Wilkins, *Considering Veritatis Splendor,* p. 53–54.

[4]See, Edward T. Oakes, "The Achievement of Alasdair MacIntyre," in *First Things* 65 (August/September 1996): 22–26.

[5]See the forthcoming essay by John Alexander, "Moral Order in the Works of Kenneth Kirk."

[6]Charles Curran, *Directions in Fundamental Moral Theology* (Notre Dame: University of Notre Dame Press, 1989); Richard Gula, *Reason Informed by Faith* (New York: Paulist Press, 1989).

[7]Hymn 82, *The Hymnal 1982* (New York: Church Hymnal Corporation, 1982).

[8]Book of Common Prayer: 339.

Section Two

The Historical Reality of Jesus the Christ

The One Gospel in Four Witnesses

The Reverend Dr. Brevard S. Childs

The Problem of the Four Gospels

In a famous article of 1945, Oscar Cullmann addresses the problem that emerged in Early Christianity regarding the plurality of the Gospels. Not only were there four different Gospels, but they often diverged from one another to a striking degree. John seems to have a different chronology and geography from the synoptic Gospels. In the latter, Jesus' ministry begins in Galilee and moves toward Jerusalem for one final visit, whereas in John Jesus moves back and forth between Galilee and Jerusalem. Futhermore, in John his ministry appears to extend over three years, not one, and is connected with the great pilgrimage festivals. Even the time of Jesus' death appears to be different. In addition to these, the style of discourse differs greatly between John and the synoptics. In John's Gospel Jesus does not speak in parables, but in lengthy speeches that often turn on the subject of signs. As a result, the question was raised in the second century as to how all four Gospels could be true. Was each Gospel written independently or to supplement or replace earlier accounts with a later one?

Various attempts were made to resolve the problem. Marcion chose only the Gospel of Luke as his authority. Even then he critically reconstructed it at points to match his own theology. The Syrian Diatessaron attempted to fuse the accounts of the four Gospels into one harmonious narrative. In time, however, after considerable struggle, both of these options were rejected as unsatisfactory by the majority within the Church. Irenaeus argued that there was something intrinsically sacred in the number four, but this explanation did not actually reflect the Church's attitude. For example, Eusebius reports that the Bishop of Serapion at first saw no problem in allowing the reading of the Gospel of Peter, but when he later read this Gospel himself, for the first time, he withdrew his consent because of its heretical content. The implication is that the authority of a Gospel resided in its content and was not tied to a sacred number.

The traditional way of handling the problem of the four Gospels, going back to a period even before Augustine, was to accept the four canonical

Gospels as authoritative, but then to attempt to harmonize them rationally in order to resolve tensions. Building on this practice, Augustine, in his famous book *On the Unity of the Gospels (De consensu evangelistarum)*, set forth a sophisticated series of rules by which to bring conflicting testimonies into harmony. First, he defended the right at times to conflate two accounts into one, or, conversely, to distinguish a difference between the two by referring to them as different events. Augustine appealed to the unity of the sense rather than of the letter. He introduced into his rule of anticipation and recollection a psychological principle by which to accommodate dislocations in the sequential order. Augustine's rules persisted in the Church for more than a thousand years.

By the time of the Renaissance, however, a new type of Gospel harmony appeared and pushed the method of harmonization to extremes. In a famous harmony of 1537 by Osiander, which was attacked by both Luther and Calvin, tensions were removed by positing a separate event for every variation in the account. Thus, Jesus healed a blind man by Jericho four times, Peter warmed himself by the fire four times, and twice a crown of thorns was placed on Jesus' head. As a result, the patent artificiality of the approach raised serious doubts about the whole enterprise.

With the rise of the historical-critical method of exegesis the problem of relating the four Gospels was greatly exacerbated. Increasingly, it was assumed that the different accounts should not be harmonized but rather judged as a reflection of confusion and contradiction, like every other human work. Then, in the early nineteenth century, the discovery of a literary dependency among the Gospels appeared to finally cut away the ground from all harmonization. Scholars turned their energy toward recovering the earliest Gospel sources (Mark and Q) in an effort to recover the historical biography of the real Jesus, thought to be tendentiously distorted by all of the Gospels. It is not my intention at this point to rehearse this history. Its broad lines are probably familiar to you from numerous introductions to the New Testament.

Again, it would be a serious mistake to leave the impression that all of this scholarly effort was a waste and can be dismissed summarily as nonsense. Far from it! One of the effects of this enterprise was that the Gospels were read with a hitherto unknown scrutiny. The language, style, and structure were studied intensely, and a new recognition manifested both the similarities and differences among the Gospels. Moreover, it increasingly became evident that the traditional way of reading the Gospels, as simple historical reports of Jesus' life, proved to be mistaken, greatly underestimating the subtlety and complexity of the material. In retrospect, it now seems clear that the major problem, with both the traditional and the new critical method, was that the basic hermeneutical issues relating to the Gospels had not been theologically addressed. Consequently, the form and theological function of the fourfold collection remained largely unresolved. By the early decades of the twentieth century scholarly interest shifted to other problems. Issues of genre, redactional structure, and sociological milieu took center stage.

The Need to Understand the Gospels within a Canonical Context

I would like to defend the thesis that the basic theological and hermeneutical problems arising from the plurality of the Gospels must be addressed within the context of the Christian canon. Canon is not a subject belonging only to later Church history, which is thought to have no real relevance to the shaping of the New Testament and can be at most relegated to a concluding chapter of an introduction. Canon lies at the heart of understanding both the form and function of the Gospels.

The initial point to make is that the canonicity of the four Gospels was not an ecclesiastical decision dictated from above, but rather the Church leaders affirmed later what had already been established in the use of these Gospels by individual congregations. In the hearing, preaching, and liturgical use of this material, these writings exerted an authoritative coercion on those receiving their word. The formation of a fourfold canonical corpus, at least by the middle of the second century, confirmed and established the Church's confession that the reality of the one gospel found its authoritative form in a fourfold witness. The richness of the subject matter was such that it could not be reduced, flattened, or expanded with pious Gnostic speculations.

There are several immediate hermeneutical consequences to be drawn from the form and function of this fourfold collection. First, each individual Gospel has been retained in its own discrete right. It was a noncanonical reading that chose principally to subordinate one Gospel to another, say Mark to Matthew, or that gave John precedence over the synoptics.

Furthermore, the subject matter of each Gospel is its witness to Jesus Christ, which is to say that its function is kerygmatic. The Gospels are not detached, objective descriptions of a segment of ancient history, nor are they biographical reports tracing the development of their subject's personality. Rather, the reader is invited to share a perspective of the apostolic witness in order to confront the divine revelation of God in these events. However, because this witness is a human response to the mysteries of a divine incarnation, the language, style, and context of the Gospels are fashioned by the cultural conventions of a time-conditioned vehicle. Just as Jesus Christ was truly and fully human, so the apostolic witness was not rendered by means of a special divine language. Rather, its metaphors were drawn from common experience, and its proclamation shared all the features of an ancient Palestinian milieu. The exegetical challenge for the interpreter lies in receiving the ability to hear the kerygmatic testimony to God's good news offered in, under, and through a human form.

The fourfold Gospel collection is not just a haphazard assembly of stories and memories; it is a carefully edited, written corpus. Although usually overlooked, this point is crucial. The Gospels have been shaped literarily in such a manner as to provide their readers with hermeneutical guidance by which to receive their message properly. When I speak of the Gospel's canonical shaping, I am describing a particular rendering of the material toward the goal of its true reception by those generations who did not encounter the incarnated Jesus, but are dependent upon the faithful word of the Church's apostolic tradition. Each separate Gospel has its own particular way of providing a truthful access to the one gospel of Jesus Christ.

Following are a few brief and basic observations to illustrate some features of the material's canonical shaping. First, each of the four Gospels in the corpus now bears the title "the Gospel according to (*kata*) so-and-so." These titles do not form part of the original Gospels, but originated with the editors who used them to shape the received material toward a certain goal. Accordingly, there is only one gospel, but it has been rendered by four different evangelists. The canonical editors provided the individual Gospels with a new literary context that maintained its diversity yet also laid claim to the unity of the subject matter. Any reading that destroys either the diversity or the unity is mistaken from the outset.

Another observation is that the four Gospels have been joined into one fourfold corpus. This editorial decision at times ran against the original form of their literary composition. For example, the first publication of Luke's Gospel has been editorially separated from his subsequent work, Acts, and both parts of his original composition have been assigned different functions within the larger Christian Bible. Likewise, John's Gospel has been separated from the three Johannine Epistles, and the apparently later date of its composition has been overridden for the sake of its role as a Gospel. Finally, the original ending of the Gospel according to Mark has been expanded. By the middle of the second century two additional endings were attached to 16:8. These additions are not simply pious glosses attached to a late textual tradition; they provide a specific canonical function to Mark's Gospel. The longer endings consist of a series of passages taken from the other three canonical gospels that relate to the resurrection tradition. In other words, for Mark's Gospel to function within the fourfold collection it had to be brought into conformity with the larger evangelical corpus. The effect of this canonical shaping is to provide a check against any idiosyncratic reading that would set Mark in open conflict with the other three Gospels in respect to the resurrection.

Finally, the formation of a fourfold corpus establishes a context that both maintains the unique witness of each individual gospel and affirms the unity of the one gospel. However, the collection does not state in advance or in some abstract formulation the exact nature of the unity. Rather, it is in the careful reading of the whole, in its exegesis, that the unity must be pursued and understood. Canonical shaping of the Gospel's structure and exegesis of their detailed parts are not identical, but rather they serve to complement each other and together make up the theological task of the sacred text's interpretation.

The Discrete Witness of Each Gospel to Jesus Christ

The Gospel According to Mark

I propose to begin with Mark's gospel in part for a pedagogical reason that allows one to bring out more clearly Mark's canonical shape. However, there is an additional reason, to show that many insights from the last 150 years made by historical-critical study also can be of great exegetical value if they are correctly used within a proper theological context. The hermeneutical issue is not whether one reads the text critically or noncritically; rather, it is how one makes use of all available insights in order to illuminate the canonical Scriptures without destroying the confessional context.

As is well known, the Gospel of Matthew preceded the Gospel of Mark in the corpus in the traditional canonical order. Yet nowhere is it stated that this order designates superiority of content or chronological priority. Because the traditional ecclesial reading assumed chronological priority, it deduced that Mark was then only an abbreviation of Matthew's Gospel, and decidedly of less importance. At this point one can see the important contribution made by historical-critical study in demonstrating that Mark is by no means a secondary abbreviation of Matthew, especially since in many passages the Markian version of a common passage is longer than Matthew's. This statement is not intended as a blanket acceptance of the so-called two-source theory, but rather it is a call for the careful hearing of Mark according to its own canonical right.

The Gospel of Mark begins with a programmatic introduction setting forth the intention of the evangelist. This Gospel is the proclamation of the saving work of Jesus Christ that had been promised by the prophets of Israel. Mark's Gospel is not offering a report of Jesus' own preaching, but rather a theological testimony to the meaning of his entire ministry. The Gospel is a proclamation about Jesus Christ, who is the content of the message. Mark's reference is to the beginning of God's saving acts, which continue to exert power through Jesus Christ. The introduction thus establishes the canonical perspective for the entire book. It recounts the words and deeds of Jesus, but the evangelist has indicated from the outset that he understands them in the light of their true significance, because Mark knows that Jesus himself is the mystery of the Kingdom of God. Mark's Gospel has already fused the proclaimer with the proclaimed, to use Bultmann's terminology.

The first eight chapters of Mark focus on the mighty acts of Jesus, in which various connecting themes have been closely intertwined. Jesus teaches and acts with divine authority. He heals the afflicted, casts out demons, and calls sinners to repentance. He exercises power over the unruly winds and sea, and is lord even of the Sabbath. Jesus refers to himself as the "Son of Man," and he forces his hearers to identify his person through his saving acts.

Jesus' mission calls forth bitter opposition from the authorities when he is perceived as a threat to the old order. Yet Jesus calls disciples "to be with him," and they are challenged to follow. The overwhelming emphasis of the Gospel of Mark, however, rests on the inability of the disciples to comprehend either Christ's true identity or his mission.

Now the critical hermeneutical problem of the Gospel of Mark is why the evangelist should have continued to recount the pre-resurrection traditions in which Jesus' true identity was hidden when its secret was not comprehended even by his disciples at first. The issue focuses on the manner in which the evangelist rendered his material to bear witness of Jesus Christ to succeeding generations of hearers. Although the evangelist was fully aware of Christ's true identity—a point fully evident from his introduction—the form of his presentation makes it clear that there is no avenue open to the resurrected Christ for those who have not first gone the way of his hidden ministry as the suffering and crucified Jesus. The relation between the hidden and the revealed Savior is not simply chronological, but one of substance. The shape of Mark's Gospel thus establishes an analogy between the first generation of disciples, who experienced Christ in his hidden revelation, and every successive generation that confronts the same challenge. For Mark it is constitutive of Christian faith that Christ's true identity is revealed only by the way of the cross. Jesus' challenge to his disciples, (Mk 8:34), "If anyone would come after me, let him deny himself, take up his cross, and follow me" is the same one that engages every future believer.

The Gospel According to Matthew

The Gospel of Matthew has shaped his witness in ways that are highly significant for understanding its canonical intent. Matthew's material has been constructed into a historical narrative that extends from the birth of Jesus and the beginnings and continuation of his ministry to the final journey to Jerusalem and his death and resurrection. Moreover, Matthew systematically ordered his Gospel topically into larger compositional units, such as the Sermon on the Mount. He makes constant use of citations from the Old Testament in order to establish the context in which his understanding of Jesus' ministry has been placed.

A crucial canonical issue is the Gospel of Matthew's manner of interpreting the Church's access to Jesus Christ. If the resurrected Christ was alive and reigning as the exalted Lord of the Church, in what sense was his earthly ministry of theological significance? Some scholars within the Bultmann school have claimed that Matthew relegated the time of Jesus to the past by purposely historicizing it into a "life of Jesus." I strongly argue, however, that Matthew's unique construction moves in exactly the opposite direction of this theory. His fusing of the "time of the earthly Jesus" with the "time of the Church" is the decisive feature of his Gospel. Because Jesus is confessed as alive, the evangelist's portrayal of Christ encompasses, in its fullest dimension, both the pre-resurrection time of Jesus on earth and the post-resurrection time of the Church. The historical lines between the earthly Jesus and the later Church's experience of his living presence as Lord have been joined. The effect of this shaping is to provide Matthew's Gospel with a quality of transparency through which the time of the earthly Jesus becomes an avenue to the future *eschaton,* rather than a barrier from the past.

No passage illustrates Matthew's understanding of eschatological time more clearly than the Great Commission of chapter 28. The emphasis of the passage does not fall on just seeing Jesus but also on understanding and obeying the words of the Exalted One, which are his legacy to the Church. What follows is not a farewell address, but an act of enthronement in which Christ lays claim upon all earthly powers and peoples. The commission closes with the promise: "I am with you always to the close of the age" (28:20). The theme of Christ's continuing presence, already found in the name Emmanuel, now brackets the entire gospel. It promises to the eleven disciples the living presence of Christ, not only for the future, however, but as a reality that has always been there. It is the theological understanding reflected in this passage that allows the evangelist to project features of the exalted Lord back into his description of the earthly ministry of Jesus. Thus, Matthew actualizes the Gospel in terms of the presence of the exalted Lord of the Church, who fulfills through his words and deeds the promise of Israel's Messiah. By his teaching, Jesus opened the way to the Kingdom of Heaven, a reality that has already manifested itself to those doing the will of God.

The Gospel According to Luke

Nowhere is the need for understanding the canonical shape of a gospel more important than with Luke's Gospel. In the period following World War II, a group of very learned scholars, largely from the Bultmann school, raised the canonical question, but, in my opinion, they took some profound insights completely in the wrong direction. They argued that because of the delay in the return of Christ in the Parousia, Luke abandoned his eschatalogical hope and sought to anchor the life of Jesus in the past. Through this reinterpretation of the Christian tradition, Luke provided the warrant for Early Catholicism, with the apostolic tradition becoming a fixed entity controlled by ecclesiastical offices within a historical succession. Obviously time is too limited to pursue all the ramifications of this interpretation of Luke's gospel, which theory continue to persist in many modern introductory textbooks.

In my judgment, the search for Luke's canonical intention needs to move in a very different direction. His Gospel begins with a carefully worded, highly stylized statement of the author's purpose. This is a classic example of a Hellenistic literary convention, which, in this case, has been shaped to serve a new canonical function. Luke's concern is to establish how the events transmitted by the tradition relate to the present and future generations of believers. How is the presentation of the gospel affected when its oral proclamation is being replaced with a written form, by a chain of traditions different from the original eyewitnesses? In his prologue Luke addresses the problem raised by the presence of a new medium of witness, namely the report (*diégesis*), with the sacred events appearing to lie in the past and to share the quality of an accomplished sequence. Luke announces that the redemptive events have not been locked in the past, but continue to impinge upon the present. The eschatological nature of these events encompasses the past, present, and future, and includes the "we" of Luke's generation along with the original eyewitnesses. Moreover, Theophilus is to know the dependable certainty "of those things about which you have been informed" (Luke 1:4). Luke is addressing the problem of how the past events of Christ's life are appropriated for salvation by successive generations in the face of the threats of distortion that form the background of his writing.

Luke has indeed introduced a definite periodization of history that sets his Gospel apart from the other synoptics. The time of Jesus has a beginning and an end. The time of the Church follows the time of Jesus, which unfolds in a chronological sequence. Jesus defines his mission during his first appearance in the synagogue at Nazareth (chapter 4). He takes up the prophetic promise proclaimed by Isaiah of salvation through the Spirit. The messenger is anointed by the Spirit to proclaim the Jubilee Year of God's salvation: good news to the poor, liberty to the imprisoned, healing to the sick. Jesus announces that "today" in his presence, salvation has arrived. All the "new" of the messianic hope has taken a concrete form as the promised eschatalogical moment has become a reality. The outpouring of the Spirit began with Jesus' proclamation of "today," but the work of the Spirit continues throughout Luke's history to manifest the sign of God's salvation in the midst of every new generation of believers. In Jesus' word the salvation of God has entered into the present once and for all, and it has been made accessible to all believers through his Spirit. Jesus is not confined to past history nor is his power restricted to ecclesiastical mediation.

The Gospel According to John

Upon a first reading of the concluding verse of chapter 20, it would appear that the author has set down his purpose in a completely straightforward manner: "these are written that you may believe that Jesus is the Christ." However, because of the uncertainty the verb tense-"that you may *continue* to believe" or "that you may *come* to believe"?—scholars have been locked in debate about whether the book was addressed to a Christian or non-Christian audience. I, however, feel that this is a tangential issue and misses the main point of the text. This ending has shaped the Gospel material in a canonical fashion by designating this gospel as the written medium through which future generations, who did not encounter the earthly Jesus, are challenged to believe in him. The evangelist makes it clear that he has chosen only a selection of his material not to provide a biography of Jesus but to evoke faith toward the goal of salvation. The fourth evangelist bears witness to Christ's earthly life, lived in the presence of his disciples, yet directs his message to another audience different from those first disciples.

One of the central canonical questions arising from the Fourth Gospel lies in the relationship between the earthly Jesus and the Christ of faith. Essential to John's presentation is the assumption of the identity of the earthly Jesus and the exalted Christ. A sharp line of demarcation between the earthly ministry of Jesus and the subsequent activity of the Spirit within the Church is never made. Rather, during his entire ministry, Jesus was the savior of the world. Even the disciples in their imperfect faith could see his glory in moments of grace. John insists that the eternal word, who became flesh, also became truly human; he was weary and thirsty. Yet the evangelist portrays Jesus' unique knowledge as having been sent by God for a divine purpose, to be fulfilled before he returned to the Father. Yet for John, the incarnate Christ of the present has not simply absorbed the earthly Jesus. In the Fourth Gospel Jesus was not fully glorified until the resurrection.

The true identity of Jesus is shown to us through his signs. In the Old Testament Abraham rejoiced over Jesus' coming and Isaiah saw his glory. From the period of Jesus' earthly life a series of witnesses, who testify to their faith in him, are brought forth. The Samaritan woman is led from a superficial acquaintance to a true knowledge of his identity. The

Capernaum official (chapter 4) and the man born blind (chapter 9) confess faith in him. The particular emphasis of John's Gospel is its insistence that faith is engendered because of the word. In his farewell address (chapters 13–17) Christ prays for "those who believe in me through their witness" (17:20). Faith in the resurrected Christ is now mediated through the testimony of that first generation of believers. After Thomas's confession of Christ as Lord, Jesus responds: "You have believed because you have seen me. Blessed are those who have not seen yet believe" (20:29). Finally, in chapter 21 the beloved disciple is sustained in his role as the authentic witness to Christ because his witness extends beyond his lifetime and is now transmitted in written form. A new canonical stage is reflected—one that is concerned about preserving an authentic testimony with the passing of the apostolic generation—and is now symbolized in the figure of the beloved disciple.

In this essay so far I have sought to show that each of the four Gospels bears witness to the one gospel. All of the evangelists testify to the lordship of Christ and his reign as the resurrected one. All of them are concerned with providing later hearers and readers an access to Jesus Christ. Yet they formulate their testimony in very different ways as they each struggle to bear true witness to impact of the reality of God in Jesus Christ. Moreover, the diversity of presentation is not by accident, but in the very shaping of each Gospel, the evangelists and their later canonical editors have shaped their material in such a manner as to direct the readers to the kerygmatic substance of their witness: "These are written that you may believe (John 20:30) . . . that you may know the truth concerning these things."(Luke 1:4). There are many other things that Jesus did . . . but we know that this testimony is true" (John 21:24f.).

The Challenges of Biblically Preaching the Gospel

Throughout these lectures I have sought to recover the theological significance of understanding the Bible as canon, that is, as the Scriptures of the Church. The failure to interpret the Bible within the Christian rule of faith has led to tremendous confusion and to an erosion of the apostolic faith. Nowhere has this problem been more evident than in the Church's homiletical task of preaching the gospel. Yet one of the most characteristic features arising from the particular shaping of the four Gospels is the structure of the evangelical tradition. It is not just described, but is crafted in such a way as to evoke faith in every successive generation. To speak of canon is to speak of proclamation. It designates these writings as the medium of divine revelation both to the Church and to the world.

Yet there are challenges to biblically preaching from sacred Scripture. First, one must preach from the entire Christian Bible—from both the Old and New Testaments. Share with your congregation the full range of the biblical witness, including the Law, Prophets, and Wisdom literature.

Second, if you use a lectionary, which of course was originally intended to encourage the use of the entire canon, do not lose sight of the unity of the Bible. To focus simply on little vignettes from the synoptics is inadequate. Strive for a balance between the sharpness of interpreting single texts and the wide breadth found in proclaiming the whole divine economy. At some point during the year you should focus on interpreting one book in order to educate your people about the importance of biblical narrative in a book's movement and dynamic. Even simply retelling the story serves as a check against offering merely pious moralism.

Third, a sermon is not truly biblical unless the preacher moves through the text to engage its true subject matter. Only when one proceeds from the text, say, from Paul's understanding of faith to Christian faith itself, can a bridge from the past to the present be made.

Fourth, be aware of the great expositors of the Church. We stand within a great heritage. This note should especially be sounded among Anglicans. Have you really dug deeply into the homiletical resources provided by giants of the pulpit, such as Lancelot Andrews, John Donne, and Joseph Hall? I always find it particularly disheartening to hear a parish priest say, "Because of our rich liturgy, preaching can play a minor role."

Finally, preach to shape your congregation with the power of the gospel. When one visits a congregation for just a few weeks, it soon becomes evident whether or not the people have been educated in the language of faith. Obviously, if you yourself are not deeply immersed in Scripture, there is little hope that your people will ever discover its excitement.

Luke's Gospel recounts the wonderful story of the disciples on the road to Emmaus. Discouraged and disheartened, they meet a stranger who opens their eyes, and they recognize him as the risen Lord. Later, when reflecting on the experience in Jerusalem, they recall: "Did not our hearts burn within us as he opened to us the Scriptures?" (Luke 24:32) My prayer is that you will receive the same response from your congregation when you preach the good news of the gospel according to the faithful witness of the sacred Scripture.

Pro Nobis: Words We Do Not Want to Hear

Russell Reno　　　　　　　　　　　　　*"for us and our salvation"*

The teaching of the apostles is difficult. Though I teach at an institution run by Catholic priests, even there the threat my colleagues in other departments feel is a constant reminder of how uncomfortably Christian theology fits into the modern university, if at all. The biologists and physicists and sociologists and psychologists and philosophers and literary critics seem unable to suppress their fear that I represent the inquisitors, the credulous fools, the haters of reason who are enemies of the life of the mind. This same fear holds true within our church and within our hearts. We are often dismayed when we read early Christian accounts of martyrdom (fanatical!), disciplinary manuals for medieval monks (repressive!), or seventeenth century Calvinist tracts (irrelevant!). Christianity cannot possibly teach that, we insist to ourselves. Bookstores are jammed with modern theologies dedicated to reassuring us that our revulsion is entirely justified. Or maybe we read the Scriptures and balk at the exhortations to sell our possessions, to hate our mothers and fathers, to excise lustful thoughts, to resist not evil, to believe that Jesus is the Son of God and that we can be saved through his death. So much is indigestible. Of course, we can go back to those bookstores and find endless volumes of scholarly study that try to put our worries to rest by explaining the alien force of the biblical text as purely a matter of cultural differences and historical distance.

Whether or not we rush to find the latest in theological scholarship for reassurance, I think we all experience Christianity as difficult. The gospel is not easy. The creed seems to call out for resistance. Yet, however much we might experience Christianity as a challenge or a threat, we are not always clear about just how and why it is difficult. My goal in this essay will be to consider this how and why. My argument is simple. We need to realize that the real problems of our Christian vocation in the modern world do not stem from the supposed archaic irrelevance of the prescientific religious worldview of the Bible or the supernaturalism of the Christian system of belief. Quite the contrary, our difficulties—personal, pastoral, and theological—stem from the fact that Christian proclamation bites very deeply into modern preoccupations. The creed is about what concerns us the most—ourselves, in our fragility and real dignity as persons. But far from reassuring us, this involvement in our deepest fears and greatest hopes threatens to destabilize our most cherished self-images. Specifically, Christianity is difficult because it teaches that God is "for us" in a way that exceeds what we think possible and demands more than we think reasonable. This part of the creed, where the news is, in the fullest sense, "good," is the hardest. To put the matter bluntly, the problem with the creed and the gospel rests not in the fact that the modern mind cannot believe. Rather, the problem is that we do not want to believe. The creed does not say what we want to hear.

I want to begin by characterizing what I imagine is the standard story that all of us were taught. This story sets out to explain why traditional Christian teaching seems so controversial, why my vocation as a theologian is presently regarded as irrelevant, if not actively hostile, to the university culture, which is ironically the very child of theology. I call this story Enlightenment premillennialism.

> Once, a long time ago, a small sect of Jews began teaching strange things about an itinerant sage and miracle worker, Jesus of Nazareth. The sect would have petered out on its own, but because the mythologies of Roman and Greek culture were losing their plausibility at that time in the increasingly complex and cosmopolitan world of late antiquity, the nascent Christian mythic structure filled a need and flourished. The eventual alliance of Christianity and political power, beginning with Constantine, insured the dominance of the Christian worldview for more than a thousand years in the West. However, this dominance was challenged, first in the Renaissance and then with the rise of modern science. Science demanded evidence and reasoned argument, and this soon eclipsed the dogmatic structure of Christianity. The Age of Faith gave way to the Age of Reason. So now, it is simply unrealistic to expect well-educated modern people to believe traditional Christian claims about God, creation, salvation, and eternal life.

Whether one sets out to debunk or defend Christianity, this standard Enlightenment story defines the issues. Consider, for example, the way in which Rudolf Bultmann describes the problem of biblical interpretation in his influential lectures, *Jesus Christ and Mythology.* According to Bultmann, the worldview of the New Testament is mythological. A world of riddles and puzzles is given structure and meaning in a three-storied universe of heaven, earth, and hell; strange events are explained by the miraculous intervention of supernatural powers. This mythological consciousness is inconsistent with the cause-and-effect nexus of modern science. Supernatural explanations are incompatible with the methods of modern rational inquiry. In view of this conflict between science and mythology, for Bultmann, the modern person simply cannot accept traditional biblical claims. For example, the creedal demand of belief in the preexistent Son of God, who became man for our sake and took upon himself suffering and death for our redemption, is untenable. Such a notion would require us to sacrifice our intellectual integrity. Of course, Bultmann assumes that the modern person neither will nor should renounce the intellectual obligations of modern historical and experimental science. As such, the interpretive agenda is set. Either we deem the biblical text culturally irrelevant and rationally obnoxious, or we engage in the subtle task of de-mythologizing the text in order to titrate out the kerygmatic essence. Bultmann casts his lot with the latter and, in so doing, thinks of himself as a defender of the faith.

If we accept the story of Enlightenment premillennialism, then surely Bultmann is right. He is not right in the particulars of his exegetical method or in his existentialist assumptions. Rather, if we allow ourselves to treat the problem of proclamation as one of relevance, assuming that the concerns of the modern person run on different rails than that of traditional Christian teaching, then good theology is necessarily the project of good translation. What is written in Scripture—the particular words, images, and narratives—is the problem. They are a dead letter that needs to be brought to life in a language and worldview that speak to our time. Whether we undertake this project in a conservative or revisionary manner is insignificant. If we have left behind the Age of Faith, then we must reinterpret Christianity so that it might be a living force in the Age of Reason. Then the only real argument is how many of the archaic thought forms of the past need to be changed. In this argument, the impulse toward revision has a natural advantage. After all, if the problem we face is that of relevance, one of speaking to our time, then surely one can never be too in touch with the Age of Reason.

We tend to cast our lots with Bultmann more often than we think. We worry about science and religion, reason and revelation, faith and understanding, assuming that the wound of modernity is primarily a matter of what counts as reasonable. The notion of divine intervention cannot fit into the scientific world of cause and effect. The modern person demands evidence and cannot accept the authority of revelation. Such are the typical assumptions. The same holds true for biblical study. We distinguish between theological exegesis and historical criticism, between exegesis for the Church and understanding the original meaning of early Christian documents. We assume exactly the gap Bultmann sought to bridge.

In Christian apologetics, a similar pattern occurs. Faithfulness is a special existential and subjective way of knowing, in contrast to objective knowledge. What counts as a fact in theology is different from that of science. Principles of evidence do not apply to the heart as they do to the head. These are just a few of the typical patterns found in both the criticisms and defenses of faith in the modern period. I shall not waste time pursuing them. The important point is that these patterns insert the difficulty of Christian teaching into the standard Enlightenment story. Whether our emphasis falls upon the apparent demands of scientific method or the constraints of modern historical consciousness, the wedge of difficulty is the same. Proclamation, we assume, spins in a different orbit from the real concerns and commitments of modernity.

I am increasingly convinced that this is a misdiagnosis. Consider, for example, a passage from the Epistle to the Romans in which St. Paul explains the faith that will be reckoned to us as righteousness. This faith is in Jesus our Lord, who, writes St. Paul, "was put to death for our trespasses and raised for our justification" (4:25). The vast amount of ink spilt on the question of belief in Jesus' resurrection misses the point. Is the difficulty of Christian faith a generic problem of believing the miraculous, the improbable, the extraordinary, or even the impossible?

The standard Enlightenment story seems to force us to say that this is, indeed, the difficulty. But is that really so? After all, we live in a stunningly credulous and uncritical age. Some people believe that the stock market will go up forever. Others hang on to every word of Hollywood celebrities when they preach about our moral obligations to animals. Not a few folks fervently believe that only a lack of sufficient funding prevents the success of welfare programs. Others believe that the free market can solve all social problems. And this credulity is by no means a monopoly of the uneducated. The modern university is full of Ph.D.'s who believe in the sufficiency of naturalistic explanation. Still other professors enjoy such an overwhelming moral certitude that their accounts of history and current events easily fall into a battle of light against darkness, genocidal cultures against liberative communities, hegemonic practices against holistic worldviews.

In contrast, Christian salvation history seems the paragon of subtle attention to evidence. The more I look up from my books, so many of which take their cues from the standard Enlightenment story, and pay attention to the strange world in which we live, the more I come to see that believing the incredible hardly seems a difficulty in our day. However the role of faith has changed in the modern period—and surely it has—it does not seem to have been displaced by reason.

What, then, is the difficulty of faith? Even if scholars are mistaken to think that the miraculous quality of the resurrection is the crux of the modern difficulty with faith, surely they are not wrong in assuming that Christian teaching has come under great pressure in recent centuries. So, assuming that the standard Enlightenment story is incorrect, what story should we tell? What is the appropriate context for thinking about the problem of belief in our age? If the problem is not one of relevance, what is it?

In his *Journal* Kierkegaard makes a very pointed observation (quoted from *Works of Love*, Howard and Edna Hong, trans. [New York: Harper & Row Publishers, 1962]) which suggests a way forward:

> People try to persuade us that objections against Christianity spring from doubt. The objections against Christianity spring from insubordination, the dislike of obedience, rebellion against all authority. As a result, people have hitherto been beating the air in their struggle against objections, because they have fought intellectually with doubt instead of fighting morally with rebellion.

Let us consider this observation for a moment. Kierkegaard is such a singular voice in the nineteenth century, not just because he was a literary genius, but also because he had such a profound sense of the difficulty of Christianity. His most famous book, *Fear and Trembling*, meditates on the collision of Abraham, the Father of Faith, with our normal sense of sane, responsible life. And this collision has nothing to do with evidence or argument. The collision is between Abraham's obedience and every other way in which we might conceive of living our lives. Abraham's scandal is moral—how could he ever go to Mount Moriah in the first place?—not intellectual. We rebel against the specific form of Abraham's obedience. And, I might add, Kierkegaard is clever enough to see but never say that the scene of obedience and sacrifice on Golgotha collides even more violently with our sensibilities than the story of Abraham and Issac, for in the death of Jesus, the Father really does sacrifice the Son.

To the extent that Kierkegaard's meditation on Abraham ignores the Enlightenment way of posing the problem, he is inserting us into a very different interpretation of the difficulty of faith. For Kierkegaard, we do not turn away because of methodological, historical, or evidential doubts. Ours is a story of moral rebellion, of our recoil in horror, of our offended sensibilities; it is not a story of intellectual doubt or of the problem of relevance. I would call this story Augustinian. What we now think of as the standard story, the Enlightenment story of western culture's awakening from faith to reason, replaced the Augustinian story. I want us to reconsider this replacement.

St. Augustine's story is one of rebellion, self-wrought destruction, and divine deliverance. It is a story he tells in his massive account of world history, the *City of God*, and in his account of his own soul, the *Confessions*. I want to focus on the account in St. Augustine's *Confessions* of why the transition from something so bad and self-destructive as sin to something so good and fulfilling as grace should be so fraught with tension. (In what follows, I used the Rex Warner translation of St. Augustine's *Confessions* [New York: New American Library, 1963].) It might be fair to say that St. Augustine gives a rather mediocre account of the Christological and Trinitarian logic of the basic plot of the fall and redemption. But whatever failings he has on this score, he more than makes up for with his strikingly clear and persuasive accounts of the intense resistance we put up against participation in that basic plot. St Augustine, more than any other early Christian writer, analyzes our rebellion against grace, our rejection of what is for us. This rebellion and rejection have two crucial elements: a horror of dependence and a fear of difference. Even the roughest sketch can help us see that there is an alternative to the standard story of Enlightenment that might better explain our present situation.

Horror of dependence is the most obvious Augustinian theme. Prideful self-sufficiency, or better, the prideful aspiration to self-sufficiency and the many fantasies sustaining that aspiration are major themes in St.

Augustine's *Confessions*. As a child, he recalls being intensely angry with adults "for not acting," he says, "as though they were my slaves" (Bk. I. 6). Of course, we quickly learn that angry tears do not make the world revolve around us, but, as St. Augustine recounts, the educational system is based upon grasping ambition, not only for riches but also for "a reputation among men" (Bk. I. 9). If we cannot make men our slaves, at least we can make them our admirers. So, St. Augustine goes off to make the world his admirer. First in North Africa and then in Italy, his ambition moves him forward. Even his spiritual and intellectual life is driven by ambition, not so much for reputation, but for the very possession of truth. It is here that he made God his slave. "Being subject to change myself," he writes, "I preferred to think that you also were subject to change rather than I was not what you are" (Bk. IV. 15). Surely, *we* have the resources, the experiences, and the powers of reason sufficient to know that which is our fulfillment. If not, then how could it be our fulfillment? If we want the world to revolve around us, then surely a saving truth must give us what we want. But what of Christian teaching? How can we be at the center of truth, which is given rather than discerned? How can we find fulfillment under a condition of dependence?

These questions come to an excruciating point as St. Augustine's intellectual objections to Christianity begin to crumble. He comes to see that Christian teaching is far more likely to be true than any of the alternatives in his world. And yet, his vanity persists. He is willing to affirm the profound superiority of Jesus, to use St. Augustine's words, "as a man of the very highest wisdom" (Bk. VII. 18). Under the weight of the wisdom of Christian teaching, St. Augustine is willing to make Jesus his teacher. In this sense, St. Augustine is able to admit that he has failed to reach the summit of wisdom on his own. The most febrile dreams of world mastery are now in the past. Yet, St. Augustine cannot submit to Jesus as his Savior, and the reason is because of what the creed says is "for us." He could not bring himself to lay hold of grace. "I was not humble enough," he writes, "to possess Jesus in his humility as my God, nor did I know what lesson was taught by his weakness" (Bk. VII. 19). And what is that lesson? We must put on his weakness; we must cast ourselves down in utter submission to the concrete form of God's divinity in the suffering and dying Jesus, so that we might rise with him (Bk. VII. 20). We must surrender ourselves in dependence upon the crucified Christ.

Here, we cross over to the second of St. Augustine's difficulties, the fear of difference. At first, becoming different is very much his desire. He reads Cicero's praise of philosophy and commits himself to seek wisdom. He shall leave behind the mundane world of falsehood and conform himself to truth. As he embarks on this project of becoming different, St. Augustine's first brush with Christian teaching is a harbinger of his later, more painful struggles. Aflame with desire for the truth, St. Augustine rejects the usefulness of Scripture for his philosophical quest. It cannot compare to "the grand style of Cicero" (Bk. III. 5). The scripture is far too crude a set of writings. It is entirely different than what the young St. Augustine thinks worthy of study and meditation. He wants to test his mind with different ideas—different writing—but not with something *that* different!

St. Augustine's early dismissal of Scripture is but a figure. The edge of difference does not begin to cut into him until after his crucial awareness that he can venerate Jesus as a teacher of wisdom from whom he might learn, but not as a Savior upon the cross upon whom he must depend. Everything St. Augustine has learned about Christianity seems to grow in plausibility. He seems to be reaching the goal of his quest for truth. He appears to be a man transformed by the wisdom of apostolic teaching. "I no longer desire to be more certain of you," he writes, "only to stand more firmly in you" (Bk. VIII. 1). But he cannot stand more firmly in the way of Jesus. He reports, "I was still reluctant to enter into its narrowness." Everything seemed right, but it involved too much. Again and again, in the crucial time before his conversion, Augustine begs to become different. He wishes to be delivered from the "iron bondage" of his own will (Bk. VIII. 5). He wishes to be awoken from the numbing haze of his own sin. Yet, like someone trying to sleep on Sunday morning, St. Augustine finds himself saying "A minute. Just a minute. Just a little while longer" (Bk. VIII. 5). And, recalling his youthful enthusiasm for Cicero's praise of philosophy and the zeal with which he had pledged to do and become whatever wisdom required, he is now overcome with the realization that from the very beginning he never allowed himself to become different. The motto of his youth was, "Make me chaste and continent, but not yet" (Bk. VIII. 7). This had been his thought from the very beginning, and now St. Augustine realizes that he had not changed at all. For all of his desire to become different, it was a desire canceled by second thoughts. How could he avoid such a cancellation? For the more one knows oneself as a sinner, the more the escape from sin requires one to destroy oneself, and the more hope for salvation comes frighteningly close to a desire for death.

The dynamics of St. Augustine's conversion do not reassure any of us who might find ourselves sympathizing with his earlier horror of dependence and fear of difference. The conflict in his soul between the desire to be different and his fearful cry of "not yet" is resolved solely by external forces. The voices of children beyond the garden wall tell him what to do. "Take it and read it," they say. St. Augustine has only to obey, and he does, but not by carefully selecting a passage he might judge appropriate. Rather, he reads the first passage that meets his eyes (Bk. VIII. 12). The moving forces in this scene come from without. By the very form of his dependence on what is simply given in that moment, St. Augustine enters into the weakness of submission he had so feared. In no sense does he discover that he had misjudged narrowness of the way. He can rise only as he falls upon the divinity of the obedient Son. Nor has St. Augustine been mistaken about the shock of difference. Real and dramatic changes follow in the wake of his submission. He resigns his post as teacher of rhetoric. He begins his journey back to North Africa, where he died as a tireless servant of a world being conquered, rather than a conqueror of the world. His mistake was only in thinking that the dependence diminishes and the difference destroys.

If we wish to think about our age in Augustinian terms, then we must see our difficulties as stemming from a modern horror of dependence and fear of difference. We should stop trying to meet these difficulties with demonstrations that Christian teaching really is plausible, or that the biblical text really is historically reliable, or that faith really does not place undue demands upon reason. Instead, we should analyze our difficulties in the same way St. Augustine analyzed his own. At the most fundamental level, we rebel against the claim that the God of the Nicene Creed is "for us" because we assume that a dependence upon another diminishes and a difference as profound as life, promised in obedient suffering and death, necessarily destroys.

I cannot show that the Augustinian approach is the best story to tell in explaining why the Nicene Creed is so deeply controversial in our day. That would entail retelling the history of modernity in some detail, and demonstrating how the horror of dependence and the fear of difference more adequately explain important modern criticisms of Christian teaching than does the standard Enlightenment story. However, I would like to briefly mention David Hume, for he provides a delightful illustration of how the supposed rational critic of Christianity is far more adequately described as a moral critic. For Hume, Christianity is not too incredible; it is too dangerous.

Among his essays is "Of Superstition and Enthusiasm," a brief treatment of the corruptive forms of religion. As Hume analyzes these corruptions, he uses Augustinian patterns of thought. Superstition is most troubling to Hume because it is a form of life based upon propitiating dependence. To be sure, superstition is laced with false belief. However, neither the fantastical belief in cosmic powers and unseen agents that might afflict or rescue us nor the irrational anxiety we might have about life after death are the crux of the matter. Of all the Enlightenment philosophers, Hume was all too aware of the ubiquity of ignorance. His free-thinking allies lived in a world of moral certitude and speculative fancy just as illusory as the traditional "three-story universe" of Christianity. Seeing this so clearly, Hume entertained an entirely realistic assessment of the role of ignorance and credulity in human life. He did not strive on behalf of an empire of reason. Instead, Hume attempted to anchor our ignorance to humane patterns of thinking and behaving. His criticism of superstition has far more to do with its inhumanity than its irrationality. Superstition encourages a "gloomy and melancholy disposition," he writes, exalting supposedly suprahuman powers and persons above the weak and vulnerable human being (p. 3). This creates an atmosphere of dread and a feeling of unworthiness in which the only shred of hope seems to be in offering "mortifications, sacrifices, presents" to curry the favor of the divine (pp. 4–5). Superstition is, at root, a training in "tame and submissive" dependence, where the natural powers or initiative of the person atrophy and eventually disappear (*David Hume: Writings on Religion,* Anthony Flew, ed. [LaSalle, Illinois: Open Court, 1992]).

This pattern of reasoning recurs many times in the history of modern engagements, with traditional Christian claims that God does something "for us" that we cannot do for ourselves. Dogma, this pattern reasons, violates the autonomy of the thinking person, compelling obedient assent rather than free inquiry. Commandment makes us perpetual children of an authoritarian father rather than nurturing us to self-directing adulthood. Privileging Christ as Savior distorts the diversity of religious experience by pressing it into a single mold. At each turn, the objections have little to do with what is reasonable or relevant, but a great deal to do with the young St. Augustine's judgment that the narrow way of Christianity is altogether inappropriate for a man trying to make something of his life. The objections are motivated by a horror of dependence.

I cannot even begin to suggest how one might respond to these objections. However, I do hope that when someone says that the Church should not require formal confessional commitments from its leaders, because such a requirement would violate the "freedom of conscience," we can see that such an objection is best understood as part of the Augustinian—not the Enlightenment—story. The objection is not to a "three-storied universe" or to supernaturalism or to miracles. It is to the very idea that being a Christian depends upon anything other than what is going on in one's head. When we stop assuming that the standard Enlightenment story is correct and start paying attention to what people are saying, a great many objections reduce to this basic form: It is simply antihuman to think that the most important things in one's life depend on anybody or anything other than that individual person. The U. S. Supreme Court protects my right to define the meaning of my own life. So surely God must be just as vigilant.

Just as St. Augustine's resistance to grace is not all motivated by a horror of dependence, so Hume summarizes for us another strand of the modern discomfort with Christianity, the fear of difference. Enthusiasm, for Hume, describes the Christian tendency to get carried away. Filled with inspiration, the believer overreaches. In a frenzied desire to serve God, the faithful consecrate even the blindest and most violent impulses as God's will. We might say that under the sway of enthusiasm the catastrophic language of salvation that runs through Scripture takes on a personal and social reality. As Hume reports, "Enthusiasm produces the most cruel disorders in human society" (p. 7). Hume is cautious. He mentions only the various excesses of the Reformation's left wing as examples. Yet the basic theme leaps out. Christianity unsettles because it both commands and promises that people should and shall be different. At work here is Augustine's other concern, his fear of the disruptive changes both promised and demanded by discipleship. Even as he hoped for that difference, the young St. Augustine feared the pain of change; he was altogether unsure that committing himself to serve God would not set off a violent revolution in his soul that would destroy a part of himself he still cherished.

We also find ourselves anxious about eruptions of social disorder. Names such as Jonestown and Waco evoke a dangerous extremism, and the media drumbeat of Islamic fundamentalism tempts us to assume that intense belief is dangerous. However, our inwardly turned culture tends to focus more on the cruel disorders the redemptive aspiration of Christianity has produced in our psyche. For example, one can hear therapists describe us as a society suffering from Puritanical attitude toward sex. Even the distant, very distant echoes of traditional Christian teaching seem to inspire hand-wringing about repression.

If I am right about the diagnostic superiority of the Augustinian story over the Enlightenment story, then objections to traditional Christian moral teachings are motivated far more by the fear of difference than by considered examination of the sociological evidence, or by careful calculation of social utility, or by a disciplined reflection on the conditions for personal well-being. The objections are more likely to boil down to shocked expression of dismay: Surely you cannot expect me to become different! Our goal is satisfaction and affirmation, not something so destabilizing as the difference of redemption.

It is important to realize that Christianity does not dismiss these difficulties, but claims to answer them. The horror of dependence, which is such a signal feature of our culture, is based on accurate intuition. From battlefield to factory floor, from feverish political rallies to the numbing cannonade of advertising, our century has ground down many more persons than it has raised up. The fear of difference would seem equally justified. Our century has been one of final solutions and five-year plans. We can be forgiven if, like Hume, we find ourselves not wanting to tamper too much with the dry tinder of humanity for fear of a consuming fire. The excesses of aspiration suggest that we should aspire only to an equilibrium of venality, a life and a society we can call healthy and normal, even if we cannot describe it as pure and excellent.

These difficulties, the horror of dependence and fear of difference, have to do with us, with the brutality and darkness of our world and with our fragility and vulnerability as persons. Christian teaching is difficult not because it is an alien imposition of an archaic and now irrelevant or anachronistic expression of the religious experience of ancient mediterranean Jews and Gentiles. Rather, it is a flash point of controversy because it has to do with us; it is about that which is "for us." Christian proclamation and the witness of faith swim the channels of dependence and difference. The Nicene Creed is quite straightforward on this point. Jesus of Nazareth is "for us," and he has everything to do with the brutality and darkness of our world, which makes dependence such a frightful prospect. Broken on the difference between life and death, he certainly reveals rather than disguises our fragility and vulnerability. Thus, even if we find ourselves unable to accept that such a man is "for us" in a way that saves, the most resistent fiber in our bodies should be able to acknowledge that he is "for us" in the sense of being "about us." The Augustinian story allows us to see that the difficulty we face is hardly one of relevance. The so-called problem of relevance that has dominated modern theology turns out to be a pseudoproblem.

Christianity is terribly relevant, but we do not like what it has to say. This is the true difficulty in Christian doctrine. This is the root of our hermeneutical difficulties in reading the Bible. To recall Bultmann one more time, he thought that the greatest myth was that the Son of God became man for our sake and took upon himself suffering and death for our redemption. In his historical criticism, he consistently explained the textual emphasis upon Jesus' saving death as a latter editorial interpolation. But what is so mythological about Christ dying for us? The airwaves are full of people promising to do things for us. If the idea of someone being "for us" is too incredible for modern man, why does every car salesman reassure us that he is "on our side." He does so because it works. We have no trouble believing that others can do things for our sake. But we have trouble with the seriousness and depth of the Christian claim that Christ died for us. Our difficulty is the narrowness of the way that made St. Augustine hesitate. The problem is that in doing so much for us, God's love demands far more of us than we would would like, more dependence than we think worthy of our dignity and more difference than we think ourselves able to endure.

Bultmann, like most modern theologians, was right to assume that the single greatest task of theology is to show how the teachings of the apostles could be a living force in our world. The mistake of modern theology has been thinking this task grows out of a distance that separates Christian proclamation from the concerns of the modern world. The task of rendering effective the word of God is not bridging the gap between the ancient text and the modern reader, or between the agrarian values of Scripture and those of postindustrial society. No, the very real difficulty modern theology senses but misdiagnoses is the challenge of bridging the gap between what we want and what God gives us. It is the difficulty of achieving the intellectual, moral, and communal discipline sufficient for even imagining that dependence is not an assault upon our dignity, and that the difference of spiritual rebirth does not rend the delicate fabric of our humanity. Perhaps the best way to express the real challenge to theology, the real task of manifesting the living force of the gospel, is not relevance but holiness. The teaching of the apostles is difficult because it is a word of holiness, and we are not holy. Only by allowing ourselves to receive that which has been given, and, in turn, to give ourselves to the gift, can we see and know how the demands of God's love are good and joyful, rather than dehumanizing and adding to the inhumanities of the modern world.

More than Affirmation: The Incarnation as Judgment and Grace

Christopher A. Brown   *"and He was made man"*

A professor of mine used to tell a joke in which archeologists in the 1950s discover the actual tomb of Jesus. Inside are the bones of a man in his early thirties. Members of the press get wind of the story and solicit a response from the Vatican, where papal officials are agitated by the news but express skepticism about its veracity. In the interests of balanced journalism the reporters also contact Paul Tillich at the Harvard Divinity School. Hearing of the discovery, Professor Tillich cries out, "Mein Gott! Can it be? You mean there really was such a man?"

This, of course, did not happen, and Paul Tillich obviously did not question the historical existence of Jesus. The joke plays on a caricature of a theological project in which the actual person of Jesus is secondary to his symbolic significance as the bearer of New Being—as if the *idea* of the incarnation were more important than the event itself. If this is not entirely fair to Tillich, such a joke evokes nervous laughter because it is all too common for commentators to fudge the doctrine of the incarnation and drive a wedge (usually tacit) between the notion of incarnation and the person of Jesus of Nazareth.

The language of incarnation is very much in vogue in the seminaries, divinity schools, and organs of communication that service the mainline Protestant churches in America. Yet all too often the notion of incarnation that is presented has little theological substance, except as a principle of affirmation. In what follows I will argue that advocates of a contemporary incarnational theology extract the doctrine of the incarnation from the traditional fabric of interwoven doctrinal themes. As a result, the incarnation, though ostensibly elevated in its importance, is actually stripped of narrative content and rendered as an abstract principle. I will further argue that the historical particularity of the incarnation recedes into the background while a horizontalist message of affirmation takes the place of a gospel of divine intervention. Such deformities may be corrected only by interpreting the incarnation according to the grammar that governs the web of interlocking themes constituting Christian doctrine. In such an interpretation the incarnation reappears not as an abstract and one-sided principle by which the world is affirmed, but as a concrete event from which flows both judgment and grace.

The Anglican Emphasis on the Incarnation

I once heard someone characterize various Christian traditions by correlating them with occasions in the liturgical year. Accordingly, Lutherans, with their emphasis on justification, were associated with Good Friday, while the Eastern Orthodox were identified with Easter because of their robust theology of resurrection. Anglicans were said to give first place to Christmas. Why? Because of their much-celebrated emphasis on the doctrine of the incarnation.

The scheme stopped here (it was, after all, an Episcopalian who suggested it), but it is easily extended. Charismatic Christians could claim Pentecost. Baptists might be linked with the baptism of Jesus after the Epiphany. Methodists, with their concern for Christian perfection, might be assigned the Feast of the Transfiguration. But the more this correlation is developed, the more it is evident how tenuous it really is.

The function of the liturgical year is to encompass the entire Christian narrative, and it is this narrative as a whole that each Christian community seeks to proclaim. One would not expect the local Lutheran pastor to neglect the resurrection in favor of an exclusive focus on justification, nor a responsible Anglican to preach the incarnation to the exclusion of its climactic outcome on the cross. The Catholic faith is a unity, and no Christian community consciously offers only half a loaf.

Yet much recent Anglican apologetic does claim first place for the doctrine of the incarnation. Urban T. Holmes, for instance, spoke of the Incarnation as "a central doctrine to Anglicanism."[1] Stephen Sykes has observed that "Anglicans so value the doctrine of the incarnation that they use it as a criterion for distinguishing their theology from that of others."[2] Paul Tillich went so far as to call the doctrine of the incarnation the "Anglican Heresy,"[3] though perhaps this says as much about Tillich as anything else. I would simply say that contemporary Anglicans frequently profess a self-congratulatory "incarnational" theology that distorts the doctrine of the incarnation by bracketing it off from the wider narrative of the Christian faith.

Christian doctrine constitutes a sort of grammar that governs the relationship of interconnecting themes. Creation and the Fall, justification and sanctification, incarnation and atonement, sin and grace, these themes interweave and coinhere, each deriving its meaning from its connection with the others. To privilege a particular doctrine, even one as crucial as the incarnation, is to separate it from this thematic web and force it to carry more weight than customarily determined by the normative grammar. Although this web of doctrine is hardly static or unchanging, disregarding its grammatical integrity can lead to deformities in the meaning or function of its parts.

Classically, the Anglican focus on the incarnation finds its expression in an emphasis on the liturgy and in a generally sacramental outlook on Christian life and practice. The gospel is thus "enfleshed" in the communal celebrations of baptism and Eucharist, in the rich cadences of the Prayer Book offices, in a living tradition of English choir music, in the edifying use of fine art and architecture, and in an open engagement with contemporary intellectual life.

Problems arise, however, when this incarnational proclivity extends beyond an appreciation for the sacramental character of Christian life to a self-consciously elevated level of central principle. This development can be traced to the late nineteenth century as Anglicans increasingly downplayed the Reformation emphasis on justification in favor of an allegedly patristic focus on the incarnation. As Reginald Fuller has observed, "Some strands of Anglican theology have at times been tempted to overemphasize the doctrine of the incarnation and to treat it as though the incarnation were in itself salvific."[4] Fuller attributes this preoccupation with the incarnation principally to leading Anglican scholars of the late nineteenth and early twentieth centuries: F. D. Maurice, B. F. Westcott, the *Lux Mundi* School, and William Temple—figures of considerable prestige in Anglican theology.

This tendency has attained near-canonical status in the contemporary period. It has become commonplace for Anglicans to privilege the theology of the patristic period over that of the Reformation, and to claim the authority of the Fathers in making the incarnation the central theme of the gospel, and, as Fuller suggests, the actual locus of salvation. One is frequently reminded, for example, of the claim of Athanasius in *De*

Incarnatione that God "assumed humanity that we might become God."[5] This famous quotation of Athanasius and similar sayings by the Cappadocians are invoked to authorize a soteriology in which the incarnation is treated as a sort of beachhead through which the quality of divinity is diffused to the human race, automatically elevating humanity without reference to sacrifice, justification, sanctification, or their subjective appropriation by faith and baptism.

This was not what Athanasius meant. In *De Incarnatione* he frequently links the salvific character of Christ's incarnation to the event of his sacrificial death on the cross. Even the famous claim that God "assumed humanity that we might become God" is immediately followed by the qualifying statement that "he endured shame from men"—clearly a reference to the cross—"that we might inherit immortality."[6] Only a selective reading of Athanasius and other patristic figures can justify a soteriology that gives exclusive prominence to the incarnation. Such a reading is the outcome, I would suggest, of a debate about the status of the Reformation that arose in Anglican circles in the wake of the Oxford Movement, and a reaction to the forensic soteriology of nineteenth-century Anglican evangelicals. The "Liberal Catholics" carried the day in that debate, and the doctrine of the incarnation became the "canon within the canon," leaving open the way for developments that would hardly have been countenanced by Maurice, Gore, and the contributors to *Lux Mundi*.

Once it has been singled out in this fashion, the doctrine of the incarnation all too easily lends itself to being exploited ideologically. Elevated to the status of the central article of faith, the incarnation quickly becomes a general principle that is increasingly abstracted from the narrative about Jesus of Nazareth. "Incarnation" functions as a sort of theological shorthand by which the created order is embraced and affirmed. The result is a general notion used to validate Christian engagement with "the world" and underwrite a commitment to social transformation.

I do not mean to impugn Christian commitment to social change, nor do I deny that in becoming human God bestows a new dignity on the created order. But to treat the incarnation as a fuzzy affirmation of the world is more likely to buttress the status quo than to advance a radical critique. The search for justice, as well as the cultivation of personal holiness, would seem better served by the "realism" of a nuanced picture of the world that is traditionally associated with the doctrine of the incarnation. The Johannine prologue (the *locus classicus* of the doctrine of the incarnation) tells us of a world that, though it came into being through the preexistent Word, neither knows him nor receives him. The world in which the Word is incarnate is a world that crucifies him. It is a world in disorder. If the incarnation demonstrates that God loves the world and wishes it not to perish but to share in eternal life, this redemption can occur only through death and new birth. In the language of Paul, the world, while it "waits with eager longing" for its promised transformation, still remains "subjected to futility" and in "bondage to decay" (Rom. 8:19—21). To invoke the incarnation as a blanket affirmation of the world is to disregard the Johannine portrait of the world in opposition, and to embrace a sort of premature eschatology.

The Incarnation as "Embodiment"

If this general and abstract notion of incarnation is typically Anglican, it is not uniquely so. Since the displacement of a once prevalent neoorthodoxy in mainline Protestantism, such "incarnational" theology has had wide ecumenical currency. An example of this appeal may be found in James B. Nelson's widely read and influential text, *Embodiment: An Approach to Sexuality and Christian Theology.* In formulating a theological account of sexuality that anticipated much of the current discussion in the churches, Nelson relied on the incarnation as the basis for a vigorous affirmation of the embodied human condition.

Because God is "embodied" in Christ, our own embodied condition takes on a new significance and value. But what is the connection between the event of the incarnation and this affirmation of the human condition? It would seem, in fact, that "embodiment" is really a general principle that has little to do with the concrete event of the incarnation. Initially, Nelson acknowledges that incarnation is a way of talking about Jesus Christ and, in this regard, is distinct and unique. He assures the reader that "the embodiment of God in Jesus Christ is, in faith's perception, God's decisive and crucial self disclosure," and that "the incarnation of God in Jesus Christ is, in the eyes of faith, the unrepeatable, unique, and sufficient revelation."[7] But then he further goes on to universalize the incarnation as a general principle:

> Paradoxically, however, it must also be said that in another sense God's incarnation is sufficient only if it is non-unique and repeatable.... for

those who believe in God's continuing manifestation and presence, the incarnation is not simply past event. The Word *still* becomes flesh. We as body-selves—as sexual body-selves—are affirmed because of that.[8]

Nelson argues for a paradox in which the incarnation is both a unique event in Christ and, at the same time, a "non-unique and repeatable" occurrence. In fact, Nelson's initial assertion of the incarnation event as being "decisive," "unrepeatable," and "unique" is disingenuous. His interest does not lie in the narrative about Jesus of Nazareth and its contextual themes of promise and fulfillment, sin and redemption and death and resurrection. Rather, Nelson is in search of a general and abstract principle of incarnation that can be invoked to affirm our temporal embodied existence.

It is not my purpose to critique Nelson's specific proposals about how Christians should live out their embodied existence as "sexual body-selves." Moreover, there is little question that the doctrine of the incarnation does challenge a Manichaean denigration of the body that surfaces within certain strands of Christian tradition. Clearly, if human flesh has become the medium of God's self-revelation, it is not to be disdained. But Nelson's use of the incarnation as a principle of affirmation is one-sided and ideological. There is no hint that the incarnation exposes our human disorder, nor is there a trace of the eschatological expectation that radically qualifies the present. Thus, Nelson's treatment of sexuality suffers accordingly. All sexual variations are "affirmed" and the disordered status quo of human desire is embraced without reservation.

Incarnation in the Renewed Quest for the Historical Jesus

The dissociation of the incarnation from the particularity of Jesus Christ, which is tacit only in Nelson and others who would reduce the incarnation to a general principle, becomes explicit in the current rehabilitation of the Quest for the Historical Jesus. By setting a hypothetical reconstruction of the life of Jesus against subsequent Christological confession, this latest version of the quest eliminates from serious consideration the claim that in Jesus God became human. The classic language of incarnation is simply removed from play.

Mainstream New Testament scholars have long insisted that the historical-critical method need not undermine confessional claims about the divinity of Jesus. But members of the Jesus Seminar, and those engaged in a similar project, proceed on a suspicion of tradition that shapes in advance the results of their critical investigation. The Mediterranean Jewish peasant revolutionary who emerges reflects a Christology that self-consciously circumvents ecclesial reflection on the "Word made flesh." When John Dominic Crossan declares, "Christianity must repeatedly, generation after generation, make its best historical judgment about who *Jesus* was *then* and, on that basis, decide what that reconstruction means as *Christ now*,"[9] the Jesus of "then" is a Jesus who lies on the other side of a canonical testimony that is systematically excluded in the reconstruction of the Jesus for today.

Crossan does leave an opening for incarnation language when he writes that "Christian faith is (1) an act of faith in (2) the historical Jesus as (3) the manifestation of God."[10] But when the historical Jesus is shown to deflect all attention from himself to the Kingdom, and all divine or messianic claims are deemed to be retrojected into the text, and the further move is made to delegitimate the interpretive canonical testimony, the resulting "manifestation of God" amounts to a rather thin notion of incarnation. Not only does this manifestation lack responsible accountability to the apostolic witness and the ecclesial tradition to which it gave rise, but Crossan's language of manifestation begs the question of the sense in which the historical Jesus manifests God. Is such a manifestation uniquely tied to the person of Jesus? Or is God equally manifest in those who follow in the path of the Mediterranean Jewish peasant revolutionary? Can this manifestation be construed as identity? Does it correspond to what the Nicene Fathers sought to express by the term *homousios?* It seems doubtful.

Faith in the Incarnation as an Ecclesial Reality

The attempt to recover the historical Jesus brings into sharp relief the fact that faith in the incarnation is an ecclesial reality. It is about choosing to be part of a particular community and to speak its distinct language, as opposed to bracketing that language in order to get to a "truth" that is uncontaminated by the interests of the apostolic church. To speak of the incarnation is to decline consciously the pretense of a neutral stance from which to discern the "real" Jesus. In his famous book *The Quest for the Historical Jesus* Albert Schweitzer exposed the futility of this strategy when he pointed out that the portraits of Jesus that emerge are invariably projections of the writer's own concerns and prejudices. In the course of this project, says Schweitzer, "We ourselves have been enfeebled, and have robbed our own thoughts of their vigour in order to project them back into history and make them speak to us out of the past."[11]

Crossan and his associates differ from their nineteenth-century predecessors in that they recognize the impossibility of achieving a pure historical objectivity. Instead, they revel—with post-modern zeal—in the plurality of the possible accounts of Jesus that emerge from their project.[12] But either way, the result of this effort (I don't see how the recent version of the quest differs from the old in this regard) is that the Christian narrative is whittled down until we are left with "a Jesus who was too small,"[13] and we have indeed been "enfeebled" in the process. One need only consider Crossan's trivialization of Jesus and his followers as "hippies in a world of Augustin yuppies."[14]

Regarding the historical Jesus, Albert Schweitzer resigns himself to reverent agnosticism, concluding in his famous final paragraph, "He comes to us as One unknown, without a name, as of old, by the lakeside, He came to those men who knew him not. He speaks to us the same word: 'Follow thou me!'"[15] Those who respond to the call of this unknown Jesus will discover within the vicissitudes of their experience the "ineffable mystery" of who he is. But Schweitzer is still hesitant to embrace the canonical testimony and make the move from an unknown Jesus to the explicit recognition of the Word made flesh.

According to Schweitzer the identity of Jesus becomes perspicuous in a conscious act of affiliation. We come to know the Jesus who "comes to us as One unknown" by abandoning a neutral objectivity and *involving* ourselves in a particular communal existence. Schweitzer rightly recognizes the ecclesial nature of faith in the incarnation insofar as a response to the call of Jesus requires one to place oneself in community. But to answer the summons to "follow" is not to grope at an "ineffable mystery." For those who inhabit this community, that call is mediated by a canonical text and the discourse surrounding it. To respond to Jesus' call is to allow oneself to be shaped by that text, and to share in the encounter with Jesus that gave rise to the text, and which the text itself renders accessible. Simply to answer the summons 'Follow thou me" is to be changed—to be a different person than one was before and to see things in a way that one did not before. In this self-involving response to the call of Jesus, mediated by the canonical testimony, there is no "great ugly ditch of history," to use Lessing's pregnant phrase, and the Quest for the Historical Jesus recedes in importance.

In response to the suspicion that drives the Quest for the Historical Jesus, the ecclesial community can only respond that the incarnation means that God does not withhold himself from us. Through Jesus God enters human history at a particular time and place and makes himself known to those whom he calls to affiliate themselves with him. This once-and-for-all event reaches into our present, not as a general "incarnational" principle, but as the possibility of an encounter that is mediated by the canonical text, the community that forms around this text, and the Spirit that inhabits the community and, as Calvin stressed, testifies to the veracity of the text.

This self-involving encounter does not depend on a pietistic sacrifice of the intellect, nor does it entail the rejection of the historical-critical method. It does, however, require an unstintingly theological reading of Scripture. Such a reading presumes not that the redactors distorted traces of a historical Jesus, but that the apostolic witness, interpretive though it may be, is of a piece with the event itself. This witness, as well as our own reception of it, is instrumentally linked, through the agency of the Spirit, with the divine condescension and self communication that takes place in the incarnation.

Text, community, and Spirit all converge in the possibility of an encounter through which the believer participates in the once-and-for-all event of the incarnation. The particularity of Jesus as the one in whom God makes himself known, the interpretive testimony of the apostolic witness, and the self-involving response of the believer within a concrete Christian community—these three moments are distinct, and yet interconnected. Formally, they share a sort of *coherence of particularity*. Instrumentally, they constitute distinct moments in a single, divine, self-revelatory act through which the unique event of the incarnation reaches into the present without dissipating into generality or abstraction.

We have seen how a prevalent "incarnational" theology pulls the incarnation out from the web of Christian doctrine and renders it as an abstract principle that has little to do with the particularity of Jesus Christ. This theology harbors a contradiction that is evident in a new (yet not so new) Christology that is enthusiastically "incarnational" in its affirmation of the world, but which self-consciously declines to speak of Jesus of Nazareth as God incarnate.

Such a theology has a mythic, Gnostic quality. It seeks a truth that may be discerned always and everywhere, rather than one that hangs entirely on the concrete events described in the Gospels. Methodologically, this theology is the opposite of what it claims to be: it fails to be "incarnational." It does not pay sufficient attention to the concrete, the particular, or the actual. It may dissect the gospel narrative with exactitude, but soteriologically it deflects attention from Jesus. It fails to attend to the context or grammar of faith within which the theology of incarnation retains its coherency.

If an "incarnational" theology is to be more than a pale horizontalism, it must retain that coherence of particularity through which text, community, and Spirit mediate the event of the incarnation within the present. To invoke the incarnation is to speak about Jesus Christ, and not to give reign to an abstract and free-floating principle.

The Incarnation as the Enactment of Judgment and Grace

This Christological particularity does not preclude reflection on the consequences of the incarnation for Christian ethics and the task of social justice. The fact that God in Jesus of Nazareth participated in our history means that this history is forever changed, and all that takes place within this history carries with it a new significance. But the incarnation does not entail merely a bland affirmation of the world. An "incarnational" Christian ethic is determined not only by the dignity and value that the incarnation brings to the world, human society, and our own embodied nature, but also by the fact that the incarnation sounds a sharp note of judgment.

The event of the incarnation is provoked by a crisis in the relationship between God and humanity, a crisis precipitated by human rebellion and alienation. To say, as does the creed, that the Son came down from heaven "for us and for our salvation" is to confess that all is not well for humanity. The union of human and divine in Jesus of Nazareth is not some "omega point" or natural culmination in the spiritual evolution of the human race. It is an event that is sharply discontinuous—an event through which God exposes the depth of the human crisis by gratuitously breaking into the human sphere from the outside.

To borrow a figure from the early Karl Barth, the incarnation occurs as the encounter of two radically different realms that can be compared with the image of horizontal and vertical planes intersecting along a single line.

> In this name [Jesus Christ] two worlds meet and go apart, two planes intersect, the one known the other unknown. The known plane is God's creation, fallen out of its union with Him. . . . This known plane is intersected by another plane that is unknown—the world of the Father, of the primal Creation, and of the final Redemption. . . . The point on the line of intersection at which the relation becomes observable and observed is Jesus. The name Jesus defines an historical occurrence and marks the point where the unknown world cuts the known world.[16]

Such an image should not be conceived as a spatial representation of the history of salvation on the whole, as if God had nothing to do with the world until, like some renegade comet, Christ entered our orbit at a single temporal point.[17] It is intended to show that in Jesus Christ two discontinuous realities intersect, bringing into view the radical distinction between a just God and a rebellious and convulsive humanity. Such a view of the incarnation forecloses any pantheistic synthesis of human and divine, and demonstrates the gratuity with which God in Christ enters the human situation. In this discontinuity, prompted by the crisis of human injustice, the incarnation is an *act of intervention*.

We must also consider who it is that intervenes. While an enduring Marcionism clings to the dichotomy between the loving God of the Gospels and the wrathful God of the Hebrew Scriptures, the incarnation hinges on the fact that these are not two Gods but one. The loving God who is incarnate in Jesus is the same God before whom the prophet Isaiah cries out in horror, "Woe is me! I am lost, for I am a man of unclean lips, and I live among a people of unclean lips; yet my eyes have seen the King, the LORD of hosts!" (Isaiah 6:5). There is no hint that prior to Isaiah's theophany he is tormented by a sense of unworthiness like that which afflicted the young man Luther. Isaiah's dread at seeing the Lord "sitting upon a throne, high and lifted up" (6:1). is rooted not in his own subjectivity, but in the objective and all too dangerous reality of Yahweh's holiness and justice. Throughout the Old Testament, Yahweh maintains a safe distance between sinful humanity and the "consuming fire" of divine holiness. And when Isaiah finds this protective distance suddenly removed, he is understandably perturbed.

The incarnation bridges this same distance. While God's terrifying holiness is veiled in the humility of One who came not to serve but be served, the divine *kenosis,* or self-emptying, does not alter the fact that, in Christ, a people of unclean lips comes face to face with a holy and just God. The incarnation thus entails a stark contradiction of the world. In Christ, God calls the world, human society, and our own embodied nature to account.

There is an element of truth to Crossan's unfortunate characterization of Jesus and his followers as "hippies in a world of Augustin yuppies." Jesus' mission is unrelentingly countercultural. It is as an implacable judge of the current order that he sweeps through the temple, upsetting the tables of the money changers. But a canonical reading of the life of Jesus—one that declines to drive a wedge between the historical event and its interpretative account in the Gospels—locates the decisive act of judgment on the cross. In his trial and execution, a result of his own provocation, Jesus appears as the judge, who, to quote Barth once again,"is judged in our place."[18]

This dialectical conjunction of divine "judge," who is "judged in our place," lies behind the classic definition of the Incarnation as an *hypostatic union* of *two natures* in one person. Many of those who have attempted to master the complexity of the fifth-century Christological debate have concluded that the Chalcedonian Definition of 451 has saddled the Christian faith with a static Hellenistic metaphysic that is no longer intelligible. Others, however, have suggested that the formula is not intended as a reality description, but as a regulative pattern that guides the community of faith in speaking about Jesus as divine and human.[19] George Lindbeck's assessment of the Nicene Creed applies equally to Chalcedon: the formula is not a first-order truth claim so much as a "syntactical rule"[20] and a "second-order guideline for Christian discourse."[21] Without offering a metaphysical model that explains the conjunction of human and divine, the two natures formula simply governs the pattern of Christological predication.

The regulative character of the two natures formula prohibits our seeing the stark intersection of the divine and human in the incarnation merely as a confrontation in which Jesus stands over and against the world. The contradiction that lies at the heart of the incarnation takes place in the person of Jesus himself. In the seemingly incongruous union of the divine and human natures lies the soteriological hinge of the incarnation: the possibility of a forensic transaction in which the "judge" and the "judged" are one. This union thus becomes the basis for that "happy exchange" by which Jesus, in standing in our place, enables us to stand in his.

Yet the intersection of human and divine in Jesus remains unique. The theological grammar instantiated in the doctrine of the incarnation does not allow us to generalize this union of human and divine to ourselves. This is not to reject the patristic concept of *theosis,* or divinization. But whatever Athanasius may have meant in saying that God "assumed humanity that we might become God," the notion of divinization should perhaps be understood in light of the term *adoption* in Pauline language. The theme of adoption shifts the focus away from an ontological union of human and divine and points rather to a quality of relationship. As the divine judge takes upon himself the judgment that is due us, the incarnation restores right relation between human and divine. Such a "right relation" enables us to share in the trinitarian relations of Father and Son in a unity of Spirit. In this adoptive sense, we "become God."

Obviously the forensic language of "judge" and the "judged" does not say all that needs to be said about the incarnation. The shift to the relational language of "adoption" begins only to suggest the linguistic and conceptual richness of the incarnation doctrine. But the forensic dimension brings into relief the critical aspect of the incarnation as an event that contradicts the world, and thereby calls into question the various one-sided ideological versions of incarnation that have such wide currency at the moment. And that same forensic judgment opens the way to "right relation" between God and humankind.

Let me suggest, therefore, that we dispense with the pallid subjectivism of affirmation. Such affirmation offers little more than a comforting validation of the status quo. The radical discontinuity of divine holiness and justice would seem far better suited to underwrite a serious social critique. The logic of affirmation dulls our awareness of the eschatological tension in which we find ourselves judged as sinners, even as we stand in "right relation" to God through our participation in Christ. So let us trade in the counterfeit gospel of affirmation for the bracing proclamation of judgment and grace enacted in the event of the incarnation.

---

[1] Urban T. Holmes III, *What Is Anglicanism?* (Wilton, CT: Morehouse-Barlow, 1982), 25.
[2] Stephen W. Sykes, *The Integrity of Anglicanism* (New York: Seabury Press, 1978), 64.
[3] Quoted in but not cited by Holmes, 25.

[4]Reginald H. Fuller, "Scripture," in *The Study of Anglicanism* (London: SPCK, Philadelphia: Fortress, 1988), 86.

[5]Athanasius, *St. Athanasius on the Incarnation: The Treatise De Incarnatione Verbi Dei, ß55* trans. and ed. A Religious of C.S.M.V. (Crestwood, NY: St. Vladimir's Press), 93.

[6]Ibid.

[7]James B. Nelson, *Embodiment: An Approach to Sexuality and Christian Theology* (Minneapolis, Augsburg, 1978), 8.

[8]Ibid., 35, 8.

[9]John Dominic Crossan, *Jesus: A Revolutionary Biography* (New York: HarperCollins, 1994), 200.

[10]Ibid.

[11]Albert Schweitzer, *The Quest for the Historical Jesus* (New York: Macmillan, 1955), 400.

[12]"I presume that there will always be divergent historical Jesuses, that there will always be divergent Christs built upon them . . .," Crossan, *Jesus,* 200.

[13]Schweitzer, 400.

[14]Crossan, *Jesus,* 198.

[15]Schweitzer, 403.

[16]Karl Barth, *The Epistle to the Romans.* Trans. from the sixth edition by Edwin Hoskins. (New York: Oxford University Press, 1968), 29.

[17]This image does not preclude the notion, as Barth later argued, that incarnation is predestined prior to the Fall, and is the "internal basis" of the creation itself. We need not be committed to a purely remedial incarnation.

[18]Karl Barth, *Church Dogmatics,* IV/1, Eds. G. W. Bromiley and T. F. Torrance (Edinburgh: T. & T. Clark, 1956), 211ff.

[19]"There is no attempt at a philosophical definition or speculative analysis. . . . Even if abstract concepts find their way in, the theological method here consists only in 'listening to' the proven witnesses of the Christian faith. . . . The grasp of the content of their expressions is more intuitive than speculative," Aloys Grillmeier, *Christ in Christian Tradition, One: From the Apostolic Age to Chalcedon (451),* trans. John Bowden (Atlanta: John Knox Press, 1975), 545.

Speaking of the "Christological models" employed by Cyril of Alexandria, Richard Norris contends, "they are . . . ways of saying that physical models are not explanations at all, but merely pointers to the truth intimated in the sound form of Christological words: that to speak of Jesus Christ is to speak of one subject in two distinct ways. . . . What governs Cyril's thinking is essentially a pattern of Christological predication and not a physical model," "Christological Models in Cyril of Alexandria," *Studia Patristica* 13 (1975), 259, 267. One could make the case that Cyril's contributions to the Chalcedonian Definition are not only material but also methodological, and that

Chalcedon similarly clarifies "a way of speaking" about the incarnation rather than a speculative model that no longer stands up to philosophical muster.

[20]George A. Lindbeck, *The Nature of Doctrine: Religion and Theology in a Postliberal Age* (Philadelphia: Westminster Press, 1984), 81.

[21]Ibid., 94.

"He Was Crucified under Pontius Pilate"

William G. Witt   *"He suffered death and was buried"*

A ny consideration of the relationship between canon, creed, and Christology must eventually turn to the cross, because the crucified Christ is at the very heart of the confessions contained in Scripture and proclaimed in the creeds.

In what many New Testament scholars believe is an echo of the earliest church creeds, the apostle Paul states in 1 Corinthians 15.3, "For I delivered to you as a of first importance what I also received, that Christ died for our sins in accordance with the Scriptures . . ." We express the same notion when we recite the lines in the Nicene Creed: "For our sake he was crucified under Pontius Pilate; he suffered death and was buried." The "for our sake" complements the assertion that it was "for us and for our salvation" that "he came down from heaven." Soteriology is the area of theology that attempts to answer the question: What does it mean that "Jesus saves"? Specifically, how does the incarnation and the life, death, and resurrection of Jesus Christ save sinful humanity? The doctrine of atonement has traditionally provided the answer to this question.

It must be acknowledged from the outset that the traditional language of atonement theology is highly symbolic and metaphorical. Traditional discussions of atonement focus on such images as the cross, the sacrificial lamb, the great high priest, judgment, ransom, deliverance, redemption, conquest of evil, and so forth. As such, atonement theology typically centers around what has been called the Christ of faith—the Christ known in symbol, narrative, liturgy, and religious art.

However, we cannot be content to restrict atonement language to the symbolic level because this language is inherently referential; although atonement language speaks of what God in Christ has done for us (*propter nos*), its primary referent is not us, but Jesus Christ, in whom salvation has been effected. It is Jesus to whom the symbols refer. Consequently, if atonement language is not to be dismissed as pious mythology, ideology, or projection, it needs to be related meaningfully to the earthly Jesus of Nazareth; if there is no correlation between the Jesus who saves us now and the Jesus who lived in Palestine—the Jesus whose life is witnessed to in the gospel narratives—then the claim that it is Jesus who saves us is a vacuous one.

Unfortunately, it is not unreasonable to make the claim that traditional atonement theology often has tended to divorce in just this manner the Jesus who saves from the earthly Jesus of the first century. Symbolic narratives about divine judgment on sin, priestly sacrifice, or victorious conquest over sin and death often have not been meaningfully related to the Jesus whom we know from the gospel narratives—a Jesus who never held judicial or military office, who certainly was neither a levitical priest or a wool-bearing, four-legged animal.

Finally, atonement language speaks not only about ourselves and our salvation, and about Jesus who saves, but also about the God who has saved us in Jesus Christ. The metaphorical and symbolic language of God's salvation in Christ raises questions about God and his relation to the world and to ourselves, God's relation to Jesus, God's intentions in bringing salvation, and how the life, death, and resurrection of a first-century Jew can have universal significance—for all human beings, for all times.

It becomes clear then that attempts to answer the question about the meaning of salvation inevitably will address three dimensions that correspond to three different ways of considering God's saving work in Jesus Christ—the symbolic/narrative, the historical, and the ontological. Light can be shed on these three dimensions by asking the further question: Is the atonement constitutive of human salvation or merely demonstrative of it? That is, in the life, death, and resurrection of Jesus Christ, has God done something unique that not only makes human salvation possible but also actually effects it? Or, on the other hand, is God's action in Jesus merely an example or illustration (perhaps an especially astute one) of what God has done elsewhere or even everywhere to bring about human salvation?

Symbol

The doctrine of atonement is a good candidate for discussing the relation between the three aspects of symbol, narrative, history, and ontology, because one discovers in theology a correlation between these three aspects that is parallel to the distinction between constituency and exemplarism, which has characterized traditional discussions of the atonement. Not just in atonement theology but in other areas of theology as well, one discovers a basic decision, beginning with one's hermeneutic stance on the New Testament canon, as to whether one understands Christianity to be constitutive of human salvation or illustrative of it. Those who opt for either hermeneutic stance tend to follow their logic through consistently. If the symbolic and narrative dimensions of the biblical text are construed as normative, not merely illustrative of element in our prior human understanding, then one interprets the text by entering into its own internal logic, not as an illustration of general principles that one also discovers elsewhere. Or conversely, the symbols and narratives of the biblical text are construed as illustrative of some previously known general truth or truths, and as subject to revision in the light of those truths. Similarly, how one approaches the symbolic and narrative aspects of the gospel texts influences how one reads the historical narrative of who Jesus was and what he accomplished by his mission. Finally, who we believe Jesus was and what he accomplished affects our understanding of God and of God's intentions in Jesus. Who we believe Jesus was for us determines what we believe about who God is in himself.

It might seem from the outset that there should be a presumptive confidence in a constitutive understanding of the effect of the atonement. The writings of the New Testament seem to take for granted that the life, death, and resurrection of Jesus effect salvation. For most of the history of the Christian Church, one or the other of the constitutive atonement models has been taken for granted, so much so that the theologically uneducated are often surprised to discover that Anselm's satisfaction model has never been endorsed officially as dogma. Jesus has not been understood as merely the best example of God's general purposes for the human race.

Nevertheless, the understanding of Jesus' death as illustrative rather than constitutive of salvation has, in recent years, become the dominant one in numerous circles, especially among academic theologians. How do we explain this shift?

First, to the extent that the constitutive models have been taken to be literal descriptions or explanations rather than models or metaphors, they have been found to be wanting in logical coherence. Just as Anselm took to task the patristic metaphor of ransom for not answering satisfactorily the question of to whom the ransom was paid—God or the devil?—so the logical credibility of Anselm's forensic account has been consistently questioned since the time of the Reformation, and then the Enlightenment.

Secondly, the metaphors of the traditional constitutive accounts are thought to be outmoded; they belong to an earlier age and no longer speak to contemporary people. Language about the defeat of Satan is taken to be mythological. Imagery of sacrifice, kings, and shepherds are at home in ancient rural cultures. They do not speak to sophisticated modern urban-dwellers.

Thirdly, there has been a shift in modern consciousness. Where ancient and medieval people approached God with a sense of their own guilt, all too aware that they did not live up to the divine justice, modern people are more likely to place themselves in the role of judge—to question a God who would create a world in which so much evil and suffering could exist.[1] To the extent that the judgment metaphors still hold sway over some people, they are considered to be oppressive remnants of a hierarchical thinking that must be overcome.

Finally, the realization that the metaphors are just that—metaphors and not literal descriptions of reality—has led some to the conclusion that they cannot be constitutive for our own understanding of God or reality. Just as ancient people picked metaphors that were dominant in their own culture to express their understanding of God and salvation, so we are not only free to pick our own metaphors, but it is necessary that we do so if we are going to overcome the oppressive and hierarchical limitations of the biblical narratives. Because all languages about God is metaphorical, none of it is adequate, and we need to express our own understanding of an inclusive and relational vision of salvation by using metaphors drawn from our own experience—metaphors that resonate with the values and concerns of contemporary culture.[2]

Nonetheless, might it not be possible to endorse an understanding of atonement theology symbolism that recognizes that the language is not literal, but is nonetheless constitutive? Could it be that the position that understands the symbols as illustrative rather than constitutive has too easily made the jump from a "nonliteral" reading of the symbols to the assumption that the biblical symbols are dispensable "noncognitive" projections of human preunderstanding?

Such an understanding of the constitutive value of atonement language symbolism would be similar to the notion of revelation as "symbolic mediation," advocated by the Roman Catholic theologian Avery Dulles. Dulles suggests that revelation is neither a purely interior experience nor an unmediated encounter with God. Rather, revelation "is always mediated through symbol—that is to say, through an externally perceived sign that works mysteriously on the human consciousness so as to suggest more than it can clearly describe or define."[3] Symbol is thus understood to be a third alternative to either a literalist propositionalism or the noncognitive "experientialism" of much liberal Protestant theology. Symbols are a special kind of sign, to be distinguished from simple indicators (stop signs) or conventional ciphers (words or diagrams). They carry a plentitude of meaning that is invoked rather than explicitly stated. The knowledge created by symbol is not merely speculative, but is participatory and self-involving. The symbol invites us to situate ourselves within a universe of meaning and value, which it opens up, and, insofar as it is self-involving, has a transformative effect on the person.

Although symbol introduces the knower into a realm not accessible to discursive thought, and the meanings of symbols cannot simply be restated without remainder in categorical language, one should not conclude that symbols are without cognitive content. Although God is beyond description and definition, God's reality is truly communicated through symbol. Symbols can distort, and they do appeal to and provoke the imagination, yet they are not simply projections of imagination. Nothing in the nature of symbol prevents it from conveying truth, and if reality is ultimately mysterious, then symbol may in fact be a better means of conveying truth than propositional content alone. Nonetheless, propositional explication has its value and symbols often require explication in order to clear up ambiguity and prevent distortion. Doctrine can set limits and provide content to the significance of Christian symbols. A reciprocal influence exists between symbol and doctrine. Symbols such as the cross and the resurrection give rise to doctrine; doctrine enriches the content of symbols.

The Symbols of the Atonement and the Earthly Jesus

How then do we relate the traditional symbols associated with the doctrine of atonement to the actual life, death, and resurrection of the earthly Jesus?

An example of an attempt to interpret the saving life and deeds of Jesus in terms of a nonconstitutive exemplarist model can be found in the work of the feminist theologian Elizabeth Johnson.[4] Johnson accepts many of the criticisms of constitutive models of atonement that we have already noticed. She rejects the traditional symbols associated with the work of Christ because they have been interpreted within a patriarchal framework, a framework that leads to a distortion of the good news of the gospel, so that it becomes the bad news of masculine privilege. The images usually attached to Christ are those of male privilege and power—he is the Pantocrator, the absolute king of glory.

Johnson rejects the imagery associated with the two traditional constitutive models of atonement for the same reasons. The view of Jesus as a repayment for sin is untenable. It is associated with underlying images of God as an angry, bloodthirsty, violent, and sadistic father. Similarly, Johnson also rejects the military imagery of the *Christus Victor* model. Victory is not won by the sword of a warrior god, but by the power of love in solidarity with those who suffer.

The primary metaphor embraced by Johnson to interpret the work of Christ is that of Sophia—the personified female Wisdom figure in the Book of Proverbs and in the deuterocanonical literature of Wisdom and Ecclesiasticus—through whom God creates, is present to, and administers the world. The use of such a model suggests that Johnson is embracing an exemplarist, or illustrative, notion of the work of Jesus, and a closer examination of her discussion seems to confirm this.

Johnson uses the figure of Sophia/Wisdom to retell the story of Jesus—to to provide a soteriology in narrative form. Through Sophia she hopes to transform the New Testament figure of Jesus into one that is palatable to contemporary Christians, especially women. According to Johnson, Jesus is the envoy of Sophia. He is a prophet sent to announce that God is all-inclusive love. He wills the wholeness and humanity of everyone, especially the oppressed and outcasts, and demonstrates this inclusiveness by table fellowship. Opposition to Jesus' message of inclusive love leads to his crucifixion, which Johnson insists was not a passive victimization divinely decreed as a penalty for sin. Rather, the crucifixion was against God's will, a sinful act of violence brought about by "sinful men," but also an act of powerful human love by which the gracious God of Jesus enters into solidarity with the lost and suffering.

Precisely how does Jesus' crucifixion demonstrate this solidarity? Is it constitutive of salvation, or illustrative of it? The latter seems to be the case.

Johnson says that "the cross in all its dimensions, violence, suffering, love, is the parable that enacts Sophia-God's participation in the suffering world."[5] Jesus' suffering is linked to the ways in which Sophia forges justice and peace in a conflict-filled world. Significantly, rather than viewing Jesus' life and death as the once-and-for-all event that effects a constitutive change in the reality of sin and suffering, Johnson says that the cross is part of a larger mystery—the mystery of bringing life from pain that is familiar to women from the process of pregnancy and childbirth.

It seems then that the figure of Jesus is viewed as illustrative, or demonstrative, of suffering and creative transformation in the midst of struggle and opposition that is going on throughout all creation. In this respect, I would suggest that there is a significant departure from the logic of the New Testament Wisdom Christology on which Johnson draws. For the authors of Colossians and Hebrews, the Wisdom figure of the Old Testament is subordinated to and incorporated into the personal identity of Jesus. Jesus is not a wisdom-filled human being or an envoy of wisdom, but is himself identified with wisdom. Jesus is perceived to be the preexistent figure through whom God creates the universe and through whom the universe is redeemed. Biblical scholars note that the New Testament writers identified Jesus with the fullness (*pleroma*) of deity (Col. 2:9) precisely to exclude him from being construed as one figure among others in whom God's wisdom has appeared, rather than as the One who is in his personal identity constitutive of the divine wisdom.

If, however, the biblical texts themselves speak of Jesus' life, death, and resurrection as being in some way constitutive of salvation, rather than merely illustrative of it, how might we be able to read the biblical symbols and metaphors associated with Jesus' saving work in a manner that shows them to be integrally related to the task of the earthly Jesus, and yet preserves their symbolic character in such a way as not to reduce metaphor to clumsy literalism?

First, it is essential to recognize that it is not possible to postulate an nontheological account of the earthly Jesus. Some interpretive scheme is necessary. Even the exemplarist Christologies adopt a standpoint from which to interpret the meaning of Jesus' life and death. From such a standpoint the mission of the earthly Jesus is no longer understood in terms of the traditional constitutive models. In the most popular current version, Jesus' mission is not to save sinners from their sin, but to deliver the oppressed from oppression. Jesus is not our judge; rather his message is one of inclusion, liberation, and enlightenment. His primary cause is that of solidarity with the oppressed.

The question then is not whether the Gospels are to be read from a given standpoint, but which standpoint one adopts: one taken from general principles or ideals found outside the text (such as the principles of liberation or inclusion) or one taken from the subject matter of the text itself. Since the subject matter of the text centers on Jesus' identity as God's Son, and the constitutive significance of Jesus' crucifixion and resurrection for our salvation, it is no distortion to read the Gospels in light of the incarnation and resurrection of Jesus. Rather, such a reading is in accord with their intention.

Secondly, the symbols and metaphors themselves must be understood in the light of Jesus' mission and identity, and not vice versa. It is the life, death, and resurrection of Jesus that provide the normative context for the interpretation of the symbols, *not* the symbols that impose a normative significance for deciding who Jesus is and what he does. Moreover, we should not presume that Jesus spent his life consciously fulfilling the meaning of some atonement model or in fulfillment of particular Old Testament prophecies. Rather, it is in the light of the life, death, and resurrection of Jesus that we see the models and types as fulfilled in Jesus.

Thirdly, it is the narrative structure of the gospel texts that tell the story of Jesus' life, death, and resurrection, which provide the context for understanding the relation between the earthly Jesus and the doctrine of the atonement. It is by listening to the referential, testimonial, and narrative content of the canonical gospel texts that we discover the constitutive significance of Jesus' life, death, and resurrection. At the level of symbol, the biblical atonement metaphors are not merely projectionist, but can be understood to be constitutive of salvation. At the same time, these symbols must be controlled by the narrative elements and the identity of the chief protagonists in the canonical story. We learn what it means for God to judge our sins in Jesus and to deliver us from sin, not by a preconceived notion of law or omnipotence (whether such a notion be an uncritically endorsed patriarchal one, or whether we uncritically reject such a notion), but by listening to the canonical story of Jesus.

In what follows, I will briefly look at three themes—mission, judgment, and conflict—in the gospel narratives, with the intention of showing an interpretive correlation between traditional constitutive models of atonement and the life of the earthly Jesus.

Mission

In his own analysis of the narrative structure of the Christology and atonement doctrines, the Catholic theologian Hans Urs von Balthasar traces the theme of mission throughout the Gospels.[6] In the synoptics, Jesus says that those who receive him, receive the one who sent him; those who reject Jesus, reject the one who sent him (Mat. 10:40, Luke 9:48, Luke 10:16, Mark 9:37). Jesus was sent for the purpose of preaching the good news of the Kingdom (Luke 4:43). He was sent to the lost sheep of Israel (Mat. 15:24). In the parable of the vineyard, a distinction is made between the sending of servants and the final sending of the son (Mark 12:6, Mat. 21:37, Luke 20:13). Parallel to the language of "sending" are expressions associated with the purpose of Jesus having "come." Jesus has come to call sinners, not the righteous (Mat. 9:13); he has come to fulfill the law, not to abolish it (Mat. 5:17); he has come to bring a sword (Mat. 10:34), and to cast fire on the earth (Luke 12:49). He has come to serve, to give his life as a ransom (Mat. 20:28), and to seek and save the lost (Luke 19:10). (This mission language is not only pervasive in the synoptics but is central to John's Gospel as well).

The notion of mission implies a distinction between the one who is sent and the one who sends, but it also indicates something about the unique identity of the one who is sent. If the God who sends is the one Jesus calls "Father," then Jesus understands his identity as Son to be given along with his mission (Mark 1:11, Luke 3:22, Mat. 3:17). Although there are elements of "prophet Christology" in the New Testament, Jesus does not consider himself to be merely a forerunner (as does John the Baptist) or one whose mission can be distinguished from his identity, but identifies himself with the mission given to him by his Father.

Finally, the mission has a goal. Jesus' mission consists of obedience to the Father, but the thrust of that mission is oriented toward the hour of his suffering (Luke 22:53, Mat. 26:45). He recognizes that suffering will be the result of his mission (Luke 17:25); he is aware that his life is moving toward a baptism of suffering, a "cup" that he will have to drink (Luke 12:50, Mark 10:38-39, Mark 14:34, 36). His mission will finish its course, and he will perish at Jerusalem (Luke 13:31–33), where the Son will be delivered into the hands of sinners (Mat. 26:45, Mark 9:31, Luke 9:44, Mark 14:41, Luke 24:7).

There is a paradox that lies at the heart of the connection between Jesus' mission and his passion. On the one hand, although his mission is inconceivable apart from those whom he has called to accompany him (Mark 3:13), and they are initiated into the secret of his passion (Mark 8:31), Jesus' suffering is nonetheless uniquely his alone, and they cannot follow him (Mat. 26:33–34). Jesus does not present himself as the supreme example of a universally intelligible principle that the disciples might also emulate. At the same time, though, he understands his suffering to be on their behalf, to have universal significance (Mark 10:45, Mark 14:24, Mat. 26–28, Luke 22:19, 22).

Judgment

A second theme in the gospel narratives is that of judgment. The Swiss Reformed theologian Karl Barth provided the classic modern discussion of this notion in his essay "The Judge Judged in Our Place."[7] Barth notes that although there is relatively little explicit mention of the significance of the Christ event in the synoptic Gospels, nonetheless, as we look at the gospel history, we find that it divides itself clearly into three distinct parts. In the first part of the narrative Jesus is represented as our Judge. He stands over and against the disciples, and in contrast to other human beings. His proclamation of the Kingdom of God and his deeds are antithetical to the thinking and being of all other people.

Expanding on Barth's discussion, we note that in his teaching Jesus proclaims an impossible standard to live by, a standard that tells us to love our enemies, to do unto others as we would have them do unto us (Mat. 5:43, 7:12). Jesus says that motives are as important as actions, that we are to be perfect as our Father in heaven is perfect (Mark 7:15, 21, Mat. 5:48). At the same time, Jesus tells us that this perfect God embraces in love those who fail to meet these impossible standards. In his parables, Jesus tells us of a God who seeks out the lost sheep, of a Father who waits longingly for the prodigal son (Luke 15:11–32). And the impossible standard Jesus proclaims is the standard by which he lives. As the Son of his Father, Jesus is the good shepherd who has come to find the lost sheep, the physician who has come to heal the sick—not those who are already healthy (John 10:11, Mat. 9:13). Jesus had proclaimed himself to be the representative of God's coming Kingdom. When he healed the sick and told sinners that they were forgiven, he pronounced God's peculiar judgment on them: "Neither do I condemn you; go and sin no more" (John 8:11). At first Jesus is followed willingly by his disciples, the crowds, and a handful of women. At the end of the day, however, Jesus' followers abandoned him; he stands alone as the Judge whose character and holiness stands in judgment on all others.

In the second part of the narrative there is a radical shift. Jesus is no longer the subject, but the object of what takes place. Those who were judged by Jesus in the first part of the story now act as his judges. Jesus' claim to be the representative of God's strange judgment was rejected by the religious and political leaders of his time. "Who can forgive sins but God alone?" they demanded to know (Mark 2:7). Jesus is crucified as a blasphemer and political subversive. The Judge is judged and crucified, and a murderer is released in his place. Jesus dies abandoned by his followers, and even by his God. When Jesus cried, "My God, my God, why have you forsaken me?" (Mark 15:34), the divine verdict was clear to all. In judging Jesus, those who crucified him declared him to be in the wrong and condemned by God.

The third part of the narrative is the Easter story itself. In this part of the story, God acknowledges the Judge who has allowed himself to be judged by raising him from the dead. In so doing, God vindicated his Son's role as Judge and reversed the guilty verdict by which he had been crucified. In vindicating Jesus, his Father demonstrated that Jesus alone was the one who had the right to pronounce the divine verdict—the verdict of the good shepherd who seeks for the lost sheep, the verdict of "not guilty."

Conflict and Victory

In a kind of sequel to his classic *Christus Victor,* Lutheran theologian Gustaf Aul(n suggests a third way of reading the gospels' narrative texts in terms of conflict and victory.[8] What we find in the Gospels is the story of a man who is battling in difficult conditions to perform the task to which he has been called by his heavenly Father. Jesus' obedience contrasts to the demonic powers, with which he is in conflict. His mighty works consist in a battle with the powers of evil: Satan, Beelzebub, evil spirits. He casts out demons and forgives sin. He links the coming of the Kingdom of God with his own person, and he associates his battle against evil with the presence of the Kingdom (Luke 11:20). In his own work he sees Satan falling from heaven (Luke 10:18). His constant prayer is itself a part of this battle (Mat. 26:38).

Jesus' conflict is also with the religious leaders of his day. His violation of the Sabbath and the forgiveness he grants to sinners as God's representative are viewed by them as blasphemy. As do the prophets of the Old Testament

Jesus sometimes preaches his message with anger and severity. His is not always a gentle message. Opposition to this message leads to crucifixion.

The cross itself must be perceived to be part of Jesus' struggle against evil. If the cross is interpreted only within the categories of martyrdom, it is misunderstood. Rather, the cross and the resurrection are inseparable. On the cross the power of God is displayed in the weakness of the crucified Christ. In the resurrection of Jesus, God demonstrates that he has power over death and sin. The resurrection is the assurance that Jesus' death is in actually a victory, not a defeat.

A quick overview of these three themes of mission, judgment, and conflict in the career of the earthly Jesus reveals that they correspond to three classic atonement models or metaphors: exemplarist, satisfaction, and *Christus Victor*. At the same time, it becomes clear that the metaphors associated with these three models cannot simply be imposed on or read off the gospel narratives of the life of Jesus in a kind of flat-footed literalness. Rather, through a kind of Christological subversion, the narrative accounts of Jesus' life, death, and resurrection provide a context that gives meaning to the symbols and metaphors, and in the light of which their meaning is redefined.

This is most obviously true of the third model, the model of conflict and victory, for even a cursory reading makes it clear that Jesus' struggle with the powers of evil flies in the face of any kind of straightforward notion of military conquest. Jesus' victory is won through the tools of nonviolence rather than coercion, and it is precisely through Jesus' death and suffering that God accomplishes his purposes. That such a victory could be understood only as paradox was one of the delights of the Church Fathers, who loved to speak of how the humanity of Jesus was the bait so quickly snapped up by Satan, only to lead to his choking on the hook of Jesus' divinity. It was also a delight of theologian Martin Luther, who contrasted the *theologia crucis*—God's power hidden in the weakness of the cross— with the *theologia gloriae*, which, Luther suspected, was preferred by most theologians.

The narrative subversion and reinterpretation of the symbols is also evident, however, in the way in which the texts tease new understandings out of the themes of mission and judgment, metaphors that often have been taken more literally by advocates of the exemplarist or satisfaction models of atonement. Thus, one might well be tempted to read the account of Jesus' mission as that of a prophet, a reading that fits well into exemplarist (and nonconstitutive) readings of the atonement. However, a more careful reading forces the conclusion that Jesus so identified himself with his mission that one can no longer distinguish between who Jesus is and what he does. His obedience to his Father is so oriented toward the hour of his death that one cannot view the crucifixion as an unfortunate incident that is merely illustrative of how evil always reacts to the presence of goodness. Rather, the self-identification of Jesus with his mission pushes an exemplarist model in the direction of incarnation. In light of the structure of the narrative, it will not do simply to say that Jesus is the supreme instance of God's love for humanity, for that was not Jesus' own understanding of his mission; rather, it becomes necessary to speak of Jesus' life, death, and resurrection as providing the very means to make our salvation possible. If Jesus' mission is understood in terms of exemplarism, it must be a sacramental exemplarism of solidarity in which sinners are incorporated into the Christ event. Jesus is exemplar as the archetype of our salvation, not as the prototype.

Similarly, the gospel narratives fulfill and subvert the forensic imagery that is associated with Anselm's model of the atonement as satisfaction, both by its defenders and those who reject the model outright as oppressive legalism. As Karl Barth has pointed out, if we wish to know the meaning of God's judgment, we must first listen to the story of Jesus. In so doing, we may discover that God's notions of judgment do not necessarily correspond to ours. Jesus' message of judgment flies in the face of conventional wisdoms. By his example he pronounces judgment on those who consider themselves righteous, and at the same time he pronounces acquittal on those we often presume to be guilty. It is too simple of a reading though to just align Jesus with the oppressed and oppose him to the oppressors, as is often done these days. Although the Jesus of the gospel narratives throws in his lot with the "sinners," his message is not one of simple inclusiveness. The good news is precisely for those who recognize their need of a Savior, the sick who need a physician. Although Jesus dies on behalf of others, he is alone in bearing the judgment for sin. He is crucified—not the sinners.

In the narrative structure of the canonical texts, it is the life and teachings of this Jewish rabbi by which his contemporaries are judged, and by which the reader is invited to judge himself or herself. And, of course, the contemporary reader fails to live up to this standard, even as did Jesus' contemporaries. We do not love our enemies. We judge others, even though we would rather they not judge us. Jesus exposes the root sin by which we judge others by himself becoming the victim of that judgment. Nonetheless, the cross and resurrection of Jesus do not mean that now we must be judged as those who have crucified God. By a strange paradox of the divine logic, the cross means (in the evocative expression of Karl Barth) that our Judge has now been judged in our place.

Salvation and Ontology

A basic principle of the contemporary revival in Trinitarian theology, inaugurated with Karl Barth's *Church Dogmatics 1/1*, is that God is in himself who he is in his revelation. The same principle is reflected in Karl Rahner's dictum that the economic Trinity is the immanent Trinity, and vice versa.[9] Although there have been quarrels about the particular details of Barth's or Rahner's formulations, the principle has been recognized as sound. The point of the doctrine of the Trinity is not to engage in abstruse speculation about the inner dynamics of God's being, but to reiterate that God's revelation in Christ is a revelation of who God truly is. God is Trinity in himself because God's revelation of himself as Father, Son, and Holy Spirit in the history of Israel, Jesus of Nazareth, and the Church is a true revelation of his being and character.

The same principles hold true, I would suggest, in soteriology. If the symbols, metaphors, and narratives that speak of God's salvation in Christ are normative for our understanding of God's purposes, and if God has truly acted in a constitutive manner to bring about salvation in the life, crucifixion, and resurrection of the earthly Jesus, then God's revelation in Christ is a true revelation of his being and character. Theology cannot refuse to ask who God and Christ must be in themselves if God has acted in this constitutive manner. In other words, metaphors and history lead irrevocably to ontology.

Conversely, if the metaphors that speak of God's action in Christ are merely instrumentalist and projectionist, and we can accordingly choose other metaphors and symbols more to our tastes, and if God's revelation in Jesus is illustrative rather than constitutive of our salvation, then it follows just as irrevocably that God's action in Christ (whatever we might construe that to be) cannot provide a true or definitive revelation of God's being and character.

Lest such a criticism of the exemplarist stance seem too severe, it needs to be emphasized that this conclusion is one that is willingly embraced by its advocates. Sallie McFague, one of the chief advocates, has claimed: "I see no way that assumptions concerning the inner nature of God are possible." The agnostic refusal to consider that divine revelation says anything about God's inner being is characteristic not only of McFague but also of such theologians as Catherine LaCugna and Elizabeth Johnson.[10] Johnson is more ambigious than McFague or LaCugna. Although she embraces a radical understanding of the *via negativa,* and an instrumentalist notion of symbol that should lead to a complete agnosticism about God's inner nature, Johnson nonetheless wants to suggest some validity to the notion of an immanent Trinity. (Oddly, Johnson seems to think that her agnostic approach is traditional Thomist theology, but she does not distinguish carefully enough between Thomas Aquinas's assertion that God is incomprehensible—shared by the tradition in general—and her own assertion that God's nature is completely unknowable.) On such an instrumentalist understanding of the biblical symbols, it is not clear whether the symbols refer to God or to our ideas and experiences of God.[11]

Johnson's discussion on how salvation is mediated after the time of the earthly Jesus is similarly ambiguous. Fearing a "naíve physicalism that would collapse the totality of Christ into the human man Jesus," Johnson confusingly blurs the distinction between Jesus and the Church. She reinterprets Paul's metaphor of the body of Christ to mean that the symbol of Christ cannot be restricted to the historical Jesus, but signifies all those who are part of the community of disciples.[12] Given such an understanding of the mediation of salvation, it is not necessary to speculate about God in himself, or such theological curiosities as how the risen Christ communicates his life to the Christian community. Once again, however, God's revelation in Christ is not construed as uniquely constitutive of salvation, but seems to be symbolic of that which is really happening elsewhere. Ironically, the end result is that a theology starting with an exemplarist model of God's revelation in Jesus ends up with an understanding of revelation that is not particularly revealing of God. The Christ symbol becomes an instrument to illustrate that which should in principle be known and experienced elsewhere as well. If the modern Trinitarian revival has insisted that God must be in himself who he is in his revelation, the agnostic conclusion of the instrumentalist understanding of biblical symbols is that God is not *in se* who he is in his revelation.

If, however, God's revelation in Christ is indeed true to his being and character, and if God's saving work in Christ is truly constitutive of our salvation, then we rightly must address the questions of who God and Christ must be in themselves if they are to effect the salvation of sinful humanity. The following seem to be implications of an understanding of the atonement as constitutive of salvation.

First, we must speak of the identity of the incarnate, crucified, and risen Lord Jesus Christ as the second person of the Trinity in hypostatic union with deity and humanity. It is because the personal identity of Jesus Christ is that of God that he is able to save. Accordingly, the revelation of God in Christ is the self-revelation of God. Relation with the incarnate Lord draws us into relation with God himself. The word of grace and forgiveness that Jesus brings to us is God's word of forgiveness. The life and regeneration that Christ communicates to us is the life of God, not merely that of a Godlike or God-filled creature.[13]

Furthermore, the cross reveals the Trinitarian dimensions of God's revelation in Christ as the Father, in love, gives his Son to the world. Although experiencing the abandonment of the divine presence in the agony of the passion, Jesus is still united to his Father by the Spirit, which eternally proceeds from Father and Son as their mutual love.[14] In light of the cross, the question of theodicy becomes muted, for now we find ourselves asking not how God can allow evil in a world that he has created good, but rather how God can allow himself to be humiliated as he is betrayed by his own creation. As Barth has said so well, it is "in this humiliation [that] God is supremely God, . . . in this death [that] He is supremely alive, [and that] He has maintained and revealed His deity in the passion of this man as His eternal Son."[15] A constitutive understanding of the atonement thus promises to be truly revelatory of God's character and being in a way that merely exemplarist models cannot.

The danger here, of course, is to associate salvation either with the divine nature as such or with Jesus Christ as the second person of the Trinity, irrespective of the incarnation, the crucifixion, and the continuing significance of his risen humanity. Then, what is seen as important about Jesus is that he is God, and his humanity ceases to have significance for our salvation, especially after the resurrection. This is a tendency particularly in Western views of the atonement, which sometimes focus on Jesus' death apart from this resurrection; in extreme Protestant views, which interpret justification as "merely forensic"; and in liberal Protestant (and Catholic) views, which suggest a "spiritual" (understood as nonmaterial) rather than, or in contrast to, a "bodily" resurrection of Jesus. The personal identity of Jesus Christ as the second person of the Triune deity needs to be correlated with the continuing humanity of Jesus Christ even (or especially) in his resurrection and ascension.

Secondly, if redemption is truly to address the situation of fallen humanity, it is not sufficient for God's address to humanity to be merely a word of enlightenment or a forensic declaration of pardon from guilt. The fallen human situation is such that it needs to be transformed from within. We do not need merely to be inspired or declared to be righteous, but we must actually become so. What is needed is not enlightenment and pardon alone, but re-creation and transformation, an undoing of evil itself.

Accordingly, the humanity of Jesus is as central to the doctrine of redemption as is his deity. If Christ is going to overcome the effects of sin on human nature, he must be able to do so from within, taking on himself the consequences of our human sinfulness and transforming evil to good. At the same time, if God's revelation in Jesus is to be a true communication of his life—not only a divine word—to human beings, then that life must be communicated in a manner in which human beings can share. Salvation and redemption consist in a participation in the crucified and risen humanity of Christ.

The model of redemption posited here is "incarnational," and shares emphases and themes found in much patristic and Anglican theology.[16] However, we would be mistaken to separate the incarnation from the crucifixion and resurrection, as if the incarnation were sufficient in and of itself to re-create and restore sinful humanity. The writings of theologians like Barth and Balthasar are particularly helpful here. Both emphasize the themes of judgment and substitution, which are usually associated with forensic atonement models. Nonetheless, this language is interpreted through the lens of motifs from patristic "incarnational" theology. The crucifixion of Jesus is not primarily the punishment of sin, but the removal of it. Sin is removed not by sheer divine power alone, but by its being allowed to work itself out to its logical conclusion.[17]

Similarly, the resurrection and ascension, and thus the enduring humanity of Jesus, are essential to atonement because God's intention in Christ is not only to experience the effects of sin, but to undo them, and to transform and re-create our fallen human nature by allowing us to participate in the resurrection life of his Son. Resurrection is necessary to re-create human nature and communicate to us the divine life. That is, what Jesus Christ has done for us in incarnation and resurrection has affected humanity as such. Our salvation, mediated by the risen Christ, involves a real change in our innermost being. Human nature can be restored in the divine image because it is enabled to participate in the renewed divine image that has been re-created in the humanity of the incarnate and risen Jesus Christ.

Here, then, is the truth in the metaphors of forensic judgment and victory. In the crucifixion, Jesus thoroughly undergoes the consequences of sin. In the resurrection and ascension, he is victorious over sin and evil by transforming human nature from within.

Thirdly, the word *grace* is simply shorthand for describing our own participation in God's saving action in the life, death, and resurrection of Jesus Christ. If it is a misunderstanding to imagine grace as some kind of "stuff" intermediary between God and humanity, which is pumped into people through a celestial pipeline, it is equally confusing to interpret grace as another word for God's general presence in the world, even if we describe that presence with such superlatives as "supernatural existential." Rather, the problem of grace is the relation between the risen Christ and the Church. The primary understanding of salvation and grace in the New Testament is that of incorporation into the risen Christ, rather than God's general presence to human beings.[18] Grace is God's communication of his own life to redeemed human beings through union with the risen humanity of the incarnate Lord.

This, of course, brings us to the problem of the mechanism for the relation between sinful and redeemed human beings and the risen Christ. How exactly is God's saving life and love communicated to us? The solution reflected in those patristic theologies that postulate some sort of corporate universal humanity for the incarnate Christ, in which human beings participate, is likely an unnecessary vestige of Platonism.[19] It seems sufficient to suggest that we are personally or relationally united to the risen Christ through the agency of the Holy Spirit. The modern Western rediscovery of Eastern Orthodox eucharistic theologies has led to an emphasis on an epicletic understanding of eucharistic presence, and by implication, of the communication of grace in general. A "real mission" of the Holy Spirit (rather than a mere "appropriation") which would bring us into relation with the humanity of the risen Christ, seems to be demanded. Without a real mission of the Spirit, grace seems once again to be understood as simply the presence of the divine nature as such in the world. But again, a real mission of the Holy Spirit brings us into contact with the risen Christ not just as the second person of the Trinity, but in his risen humanity. Grace is mediated to redeemed human beings in a Trinitarian manner: from God the Father, through the mediation of the risen Christ, by the agency of the Holy Spirit—the Spirit who makes the humanity of the risen Christ present to us to remake our humanity in the divine image.

Our discussion of the doctrine of atonement has led us to conclusions that have implications for our general approach to Scripture and for other areas of theology as well. Specifically, the symbolic and narrative character of the canonical Scriptures point beyond themselves in the direction of both history and ontology. The symbols and narratives refer first to the historical Jesus "who died for our sins," but also to the God who was reconciling the world to himself in Jesus Christ (2 Cor. 5:19). Whether we understand God's saving work in Christ to be constitutive or illustrative of salvation has implications not only for what we understand about the earthly Jesus, but also for how we read the canonical texts and for what we understand to be true of God's very nature. The currently popular approach that seeks to reinterpret the symbols and narratives of the canonical Scriptures in a manner that resonates more with the concerns of contemporary culture ultimately must arrive at an agnosticism about God's character and his intentions for the world, for its primary view of the biblical symbols and narratives is that they are projectionist: they tell us not so much about what God has done in Christ, but about our own concerns and aspirations. At the same time, to allow a normative value to the metaphors and symbols of Scripture that refer to God's atoning work in Jesus Christ does not provide license to decide that we know ahead of time what those symbols mean. Rather, it is by entering into the narrative logic of the canonical Scriptures that we discover the meaning of the symbols, a narrative logic that subverts simplistic literalism. Theologically, the narratives themselves must be read in light of the incarnation, crucifixion, and resurrection of Jesus, and of the revelation of the triune God witnessed to in both canon and creed, for the symbols do not terminate either in themselves or in our own religious imagination, but point beyond themselves to the God we confess as Father, Son, and Holy Spirit, the God who has truly come near to us in the cross and resurrection of Jesus Christ.

[1]C.S. Lewis, "God in the Dock," *God in the Dock: Essays on Theology and Ethics* (Grand Rapids: William B. Eerdmans Publishing Co., 1973), 240–244.

[2]For an extended development of the above arguments, see Sallie McFague, *Models of God: Theology for an Ecological, Nuclear Age* (Philadelphia: Fortress Press, 1987).

[3]Avery Dulles, S.J., *Models of Revelation* (Garden City, NY: Doubleday Co., 1983), 131. For what follows, see *Models*, 131–173, as well as Dulles, *The Craft of Theology: From Symbol to System* (New York: Crossroad Publishing Co., 1992), 17–39.

[4]Elizabeth Johnson, *She Who Is: The Mystery of God in Feminist Theological Discourse* (New York: Crossroad Publishing Co., 1992), 150–169. The same material is slightly revised in Johnson, "Redeeming the Name of Christ: Christology," *Freeing Theology: The Essentials of Theology in Feminist Perspective,* ed. Catherine Mowry LaCugna (San Francisco: HarperSanFrancisco, 1993), 115–137.

[5]Johnson, *She Who is,* 159.

[6]Hans Urs von Balthasar, *Theodrama: Theological Dramatic Theory, III. Dramatis Personae: Persons in Christ,* trans. Graham Harrison (San Francisco: Ignatius Press, 1992), 149–173; *Theodrama: Theological Dramatic Theory, IV: The Action,* trans. Graham Harrison (San Francisco: Ignatius Press, 1994), 231–240. See also Balthasar, *Mysterium Paschale: The Mystery of Easter,* trans. Aidan Nichols, O.P. (Grand Rapids: William B. Eerdmans Publishing Co., 1990).

[7]Karl Barth, "The Judged Judged in Our Place," *Church Dogmatics 4/1 The Doctrine of Reconciliation,* trans. G.W. Bromiley & T.F. Torrance (Edinburgh: T. & T. Clark, 1956, 1985), 211–282.

[8]Gustaf Aulén, *The Drama and the Symbols,* trans. Sydney Litton (Philadelphia: Fortress Press, 1970), 144–177. The original was *Christus Victor: An Historical Study of the Three Main Types of the Idea of the Atonement,* trans. A.G. Herbert (New York: Macmillan Publishing Co., 1969).

[9]Karl Barth, "The Triune God," *Church Dogmatics: The Doctrine of the World of God 1/1,* trans. G.W. Bromiley (Edinburgh: T. & T. Clark, 1975); Karl Rahner, The Trinity, trans. Joseph Donceel (New York: Seabury Press, 1974).

[10]McFague, *Models of God,* 224; Catherine Mowry LaCugna, *God for Us: The Trinity and Christian Life* (San Francisco: HarperSanFrancisco, 1991). LaCugna identified the Trinity only with the economic Trinity of salvation-history and rejected any notion of intradivine Trinitarian relations (the traditional "immanent" Trinity), or that the economy would imply real distinctions in God. She thought it necessary to abandon discussion of God *in se.* In her own words: "The notion of God's 'inner life' cannot stand up to scrutiny" (209-233). Johnson's views are found throughout her book, *She Who Is.*

[11]Francis Martin, *The Feminist Question: Feminist Theology in the Light of Christian Tradition* (Grand Rapids: William B. Eerdmans Publishing Co., 1994), 221–264.

[12]Johnson, *She Who Is,* 161–164.

[13]Thoms F. Torrance, *The Mediation of Christ* (Grand Rapids: William B. Eerdmans Publishing Co., 1983), 57–82.

[14]Balthasar, *Theodrama IV,* 317–328.

[15]Barth, *Church Dogmatics 4/1,* 246–247.

[16]"Incarnational" interpretations of the atonement can be found in Eric L. Mascall, *Christ, the Christian and the Church: A Study of the Incarnation and its Consequences* (London: Longmans & Green, 1946); Torrance, *Mediation of Christ;* Vernon White, *Atonement and Incarnation: An Essay in Universalism and Particularity* (Cambridge: Cambridge University Press, 1991).

[17]Barth, *Church Dogmatics 4/1,* 272; Balthasar, *Theodrama IV,* 332ff.; Torrance, *Mediation of Christ,* 70 ff.

[18]A central theme in C. F. D. Moule, *The Origin of Christology* (Cambridge: Cambridge University Press, 1977).

[19]As does Mascall, *Christ, The Christian and the Church,* 71 ff.

Section Three

The Lordship of Jesus in Human History

The Nature of the Christian Bible: One Book, Two Testaments

The Reverend Dr. Brevard S. Childs

The Relation of the Testaments: An Ancient and Modern Problem

The problem of understanding the relation between the two testaments of the Christian Bible, the Old Testament and the New, remains of fundamental importance in assessing the person and work of Jesus Christ. Throughout the entire history of the Church, confusion regarding the role of the two testaments has resulted in a widespread theological blurring of Christian doctrine almost on every front. The issue is not a narrow problem, largely of interest to biblical specialists, but one that lies at the heart of the Christian faith.

The early Christian Church inherited the Jewish Scriptures as a corpus of sacred writings, which, as the revelation of God to Israel, was accepted as normative for faith and practice. This collection came not just as a bundle of loosely assembled traditions but as a carefully preserved and ordered written corpus that was divided into three distinctive parts: the Torah, the Prophets, and the Writings. These Hebrew Scriptures—often in Greek translation—functioned as the only Bible for the Church until the middle of the second century. Yet at no time in the early centuries was the relation of the two testaments definitively spelled out in a detailed theological formulation. The struggle to achieve theological clarity emerged when the Church was called upon to resist what it came to believe was false understanding.

In the history of the early Church the rise of various schools of thought, ultimately condemned as heresies, forced its leaders to define the Church's position over and against what was judged to be an erroneous doctrine. Marcion's teaching was judged false because the Old Testament was basically denigrated and separated from the truth of the gospel. Conversely, the Ebionite's position was rejected because it held to the Torah to such an extent that it threatened the newness of the gospel. The Gnostics, by claiming a secret, esoteric tradition known only to the initiated, were thought to represent a danger to biblical revelation as revealed in Scripture. And the Montanists appeared to undercut Israel's tradition by appealing to a spirituality that provided an access to God apart from the Catholic tradition. I have no doubt that there were also political factors and personality conflicts involved in the final ecclesiastical judgment. Nevertheless, I would affirm that these theological judgments were correct and necessary.

Still, the difficulty of understanding the relation between the two testaments is far from solved by rejecting false opinions. One senses the depth of the theological problem when one reflects on the issue of continuity and discontinuity between the Church and the synagogue as the common Scripture was revered by two very different religious communities.

Observe the extent of the unbroken continuity between Jewish and Christian faiths. The books of the Hebrew Bible were received as Christian Scripture in unredacted form. There was no attempt made through alterations or interpolations to "Christianize" the Scriptures or to bracket Old Testament books with parts of those from the New, for example, Genesis, with selections from John's gospel.

Additionally, the pointing by the Massoretes of the Hebrew consonantal text in continuity with the oral tradition of the Jewish synagogue was taken for granted as the authoritative rendering of the sense of the received text. This implies that the meaning of the Scriptures, as accepted by the Church, continued to be preserved in the bosom of the synagogue even after the rise of Christianity. When Jerome translated the Hebrew Bible into Latin at the end of the fourth century and made use of philological tools outside of Jewish tradition, he still remained largely dependent on the oral tradition of the synagogue passed on to him by his Jewish teachers.

Further demonstrating this issue of continuity and discontinuity, there was no hint in early Christianity that a new God was being introduced or that the portrait given in the Old Testament was in need of correction. Early Christianity continued to fight on a common front with Judaism against various forms of paganism. In fact, the worship of the early Church was deeply shaped by the use of the Hebrew Bible, especially with prayers from the Psalter, which were appropriated freely as the most suitable language of Christian faith.

And finally, one last point that supports this issue is that a truly obedient response to God by Christians following the lead of Paul, was defined as the faith of Father Abraham, who became the model of faithfulness to God's gracious offer of salvation.

We likewise must observe the elements of discontinuity in regard to their common Scripture. On the formal side, very shortly the Jewish Scriptures were read almost exclusively by the Christian Church in Greek translation, and the order of the Septuagint—namely the Law, History, Wisdom, and Prophets, including Daniel—was adopted. This shift did not arise so much from a conscious hermeneutical decision, but rather because Christians found the Greek order of the Prophets, when assigned to the end of the canon, a more compatible bridge from the Old Testament to the New. Clearly, Christians also reflected a different attitude than Jews regarding the sacred quality of Hebrew as a language. Moreover, in addition to using a Greek translation of the Hebrew, Christians very shortly accepted as sacred books those contained in the Septuagint, but not those in the Hebrew. This in time set the stage for the subsequent debate within Christianity over the authority of the so-called apocryphal books.

On the more material side, a sharp discontinuity emerged in very use of the nomenclature in an Old Testament, which of course implied that its authoritative place was now shared within the larger context of a New Testament. Additionally, there was a paralleled development within Judaism that further exacerbated the sense of alienation. The Jewish reading of the Hebrew Bible was increasingly placed within the larger context of rabbinical tradition—the Targums, Mishnah, Midrashim, and Talmuds. The effect was that the voice of the Hebrew Bible was heard in concert with two additional collections of sacred tradition by two separate communities. In terms of the Christian Church, the result of the development of the evangelical tradition leading to the formation of a New Testament was a shift in the dominant theological categories used as hermeneutical guides. The rubrics of prophecy and fulfillment, of law and gospel, and of word and Spirit served to effect a very different hearing of those sacred writings held in common.

Another important difference between the reading of the Scriptures common to the synagogue and the Church can be characterized by the rubric "letter and spirit." In 2 Corinthians 3 Paul describes the ministry of the new covenant as one of the Spirit, not of the letter. Later, he speaks of "the letter which kills, but the Spirit which gives life" (2 Cor. 3:6). Here the difference lies not in the scope of Scripture, but in its function. The early Church, following the lead of Paul, argued that the biblical text in itself was not life-giving, but was only the vehicle for the Spirit, who is the source of life. Even the sacred text, without the Spirit's illumination of its true subject matter, could be deadening. By the time of Justin Martyr it had become a standard part of the Christian apologetic that the Jews understood the Scriptures "legalistically"—they focused on the external side of the letter but failed to penetrate to its spiritual center.

If the early Church struggled to interpret its understanding of the relation of the Christian Bible's two testaments, the problem has only increased in difficulty during the modern history of the Church. Many complicated cultural and intellectual issues have further exacerbated the problem. Following, just briefly listed, are a few of the problems.

The tendency to subordinate the Old Testament first articulated by Marcion has always attracted groups within the Church. Particularly from the side of the Protestant wing of the "Free Church," the rubric, "saved by grace alone," seemed to imply that the New Testament had fully replaced the Old. As a consequence, one often reads even in creedal statements that the Church's authoritative guide is that of the New Testament, in the teachings and example of Jesus.

On the other hand, the exact opposite problem has plagued the Reformed wing of the Church: legalism. Calvinism, when filtered through English and New England Puritan theology, often fell prey to the temptation of turning gospel into law. Much of New England's early history can be explained as the people's way to escape from the Old Testament through various forms of Unitarianism, which substituted for it an appeal to reason and personal religious experience.

Finally, in the Victorian Age the growth of the science of comparative religion, epitomized in the English-speaking world by James Frazer's *The Golden Bough,* brought the categories of evolution to bear on the interpretation of the Bible, thus relegating the Old Testament to a primitive stage of human growth no longer suitable for an enlightened age.

Today one senses that all of these influences are at work in modern debates over questions of political correctness. Is it offensive to Jews when others refer to the Jewish Scriptures as the Old Testament? Many Presbyterians, especially, have resorted to the terminology of "our Hebrew Bible plus a New Testament." The effect of this solution, however, is to shatter the traditional unity of the Christian Bible. Additionally, it doesn't seem possible to adopt the suggested terminology of a first and second testament without flattening an important Christian theological distinction by such a neutral terminology. Clearly the present confusion and embarrassment over traditional Christian terminology are symptomatic only of a far deeper level of perplexity regarding the essential nature of the Christian Bible with its Old and New Testaments.

Some Reflections on a Way out of the Impasse

One fruitful place with which to begin in seeking a theological resolution of the problem is a study of the actual role of the Old Testament in shaping the New Testament. The formation of the Christian Church did not begin with a scholarly study of the Old Testament. The early Christian disciples were not trained Jewish scribes and sages. Rather, the whole witness of the New Testament makes it clear that the Church came into being from the explosive power exerted by the life, death, and resurrection of Jesus in the lives of men and women. From every page of the Gospels one reads of the impact of Jesus, who in every way was a human being, a man, and a Jew— speaking Aramaic and living in Palestine under Roman oppression—who appeared to many to be simply the son of a carpenter. And yet he caused those whom he met to respond, "No one ever spoke as this man" (John 7:46), "To whom shall we go, you have the words of eternal life" (John 6:68), "Depart from me for I am a sinful man." (Luke 5:8),"Who is, this that even the winds and water heed his command?" (Mark 4:41). Jesus was the one who called forth the confession of Peter, "Thou are the Christ, the Son of the Living God" (Matthew 16:16), and the response of Thomas, "My Lord and my God" (John 20:28). The overwhelming reaction that brought the Church into being was the evidence of a radical, divine newness through Jesus' presence. Paul formulated theologically this consensus, "If anyone is in Christ, behold a new creation, the old has passed, all things have become new" (2 Cor. 5:17).

Yet what is remarkable, indeed crucial, to our reflection is that very shortly it became clear to the writers of the New Testament that the figure of Jesus and his divine mission as sent from God could be correctly understood only if Jesus were understood in relation to the plan of God revealed in the Old Testament to his chosen people. Without the setting of the Old Testament, Jesus of Nazareth could be seen as simply a miracle worker, an ecstatic prophet, a political revolutionary, or a disturbed Jewish fanatic. The list of identifications is limitless.

Therefore, it was not by chance that the witness to Jesus Christ in the New Testament was shaped by the study of the Old Testament. His very name, Jesus Christ, sounded immediately the heart of the gospel. Jesus was God's promised Messiah to Israel. His life and death were not some heroic venture ending in martyrdom, but the entrance of God incarnate, who bore the sins of his people to bring atonement, forgiveness, and redemption to a lost and rebellious creation, and through whom the kingdom of God entered in power by the resurrection.

Because Jesus Christ was understood fully by means of Old Testament language and imagery, it is at times difficult to separate the actual historical description of Christ's passion and death from the typological portrayal of suffering Israel, calling to God for deliverance and slowly being drawn into the depths of the underworld. Recall this description in Matthew 27:33–46: "They led him away to crucify him and they came to Golgotha (The Place of the Skull).... When they crucified him, they divided his garments among them and over his head they put the charge 'Jesus, the king of the Jews.'... And there was darkness over the land and at the ninth hour Jesus cried out [the words are from Psalm 22] 'My God, my God, why hast thou forsaken me?'" Like generations of suffering Israelites, Jesus cried out, yielding up his spirit, and the curtain of the temple was rent in two. The earth shook and the tombs were opened and many bodies of the saints were raised.

In his well-known book, *The Riddle of the New Testament*, Edwin Hoskyns puzzled over the fact that the Old and the New Testaments were so closely fused in the four Gospels that a clean separation seemed impossible. The point is that the New Testament was not attempting to describe an isolated event within history, but a moment in God's history that encompassed the life of all Israel and that gave meaning to the whole of creation in its ultimate purpose. Surely the incarnation in time and space was central, but God's salvation in Christ was somehow already adumbrated in his redemption of Israel, which was testified to in the Scriptures of the Old Testament.

The life, death, and resurrection of Jesus Christ unveiled the entire Old Testament as the revelation of God for the redemption of the world, but conversely the Old Testament was the vehicle by which the redemptive events of the gospel received their true meaning. Therefore, the relation between the testaments remains dialectical. The completely New Testament of the gospel is formulated in the terms of the Old. Herein lies the deep mystery surrounding the two testaments. Separate, yet undivided. Two voices, yet the sound is similar. An old word pointing to the new, yet the new is only known in the old. St. Augustine's formulation is familiar: "In the Old Testament, the New is concealed; in the New the Old is revealed." (*Quaestiones in Heptateuchum* 2, 73, CCL33, 106, 1279f.) My former homiletics teacher at Princeton, Andrew Blackwood, put it this way, "The best part of the Bible is the Old Testament, except for the New."

In conclusion, I think that if one begins to reflect theologically, following the leads of the great theologians of the Church, it becomes immediately evident why so much of the recent work in the so-called 'Third Quest for the Historical Jesus" is so deeply flawed from the outset. First of all, very few of those engaged in this modern enterprise take seriously the Old Testament context of the Gospels. Of course many would vigorously deny this, but what they find in their Old Testament/Jewish research provides merely historical, cultural, and literary background. The theological dimension of the Old Testament itself is basically ignored.

Furthermore, the attempts to bring to bear the modern Enlightenment categories of historicity function much like a color-blind man trying to describe the paintings of Vincent van Gogh. The reality of human history is far too multifaceted to be encompassed within the categories of human rationality. This also explains why the Church needed the witness of all four Gospels and not just one in order to even begin to capture the richness of the events that had occurred.

And most importantly, there is a basic epistemological issue at stake. The gospel writers constantly make it clear that the person and work of Jesus were such that his identity and mystery were both revealed and concealed. Knowledge of the truth was tied to faithful response. For some who encountered Jesus of Nazareth, he remained a carpenter's son: "Do we not know his brothers and sisters?" Yet others confessed, "We have heard, seen with our eyes, looked upon and touched with our hands, the eternal life made manifest" (1 John 7f). This one to whom they testified was not just a figure of the past to be somehow recovered through critical techniques; rather he is "the Son sent from God into the world that we may continue to live in him. . . . He has given to us understanding which is true" (1 John 4:9;5:20)

Levels of Meaning in the Interpretation of the Bible

Up to this point in seeking to describe the relationship between the two testaments, I have tried to indicate an apparent paradox. On the one hand, the canonical form of the Christian Bible with its two testaments provides the grounds for respecting the two discrete voices according to the literal, or plain, sense of the text. On the other hand, the Christian Church has always affirmed that Scripture offers a unified witness bearing testimony to one Lord, Jesus Christ, who is the divine reality undergirding the entire biblical canon. How can these two statements be reconciled?

I would like now to defend the need for a multilevel reading of Scripture according to different contexts. I am not suggesting for a moment that we merely return to a traditional fourfold interpretive scheme of the Middle Ages, which continually dissolved the biblical text into fanciful allegory. Different levels were dealt with frequently in an arbitrary manner, which resulted in fragmenting the text's unity. The integral connection of text and substance was seriously blurred, and the theological content was lost in a mass of disconnected observations. For these reasons, the Protestant reformers became increasingly critical of the traditional form of exegesis, and they argued that the clear, unequivocal voice of Scripture was compromised by a din of dissonant notes. Nevertheless, in spite of its shortcomings, traditional medieval exegesis correctly sensed the need for interpreting Scripture in ways that did justice to its rich diversity in addressing different contexts, and in serving a variety of functions when instructing the Church in the ways of God.

In proposing a multilevel approach to the Bible, I am suggesting a single method of interpretation that takes seriously both the different dimensions constituting the biblical text and the different contexts in which the text operates. There is no fixed temporal order in exegesis or the priority of one avenue of entrance over another. The test of success lies in the ability of an interpretation to illuminate the full range of the senses of the text while holding together textual witness and subject matter in a unity commensurate with its canonical function. For pedagogical clarity, however, I shall outline three exegetical points of entry, but the unity of one interpretation is assumed throughout.

In order to hear the voice of the Old Testament witness in its own right, it is essential to interpret each passage within its historical, literary, and canonical contexts. For example, if one is dealing seriously with the Old Testament genre of narrative, then to read the person of Jesus Christ back into the story say, wrestling with Jacob at the river Jabbok (Genesis 32), is to distort the text's testimony and to drown out the Old Testament's own voice. On the story level one cannot fuse promise and fulfillment. In classic terminology, the appeal is to the *sensus literalis,* literary sense, of the Scriptures. However, even when restricting oneself to the Hebrew Bible according to its canonical shape, the serious interpreter is still constrained to relate the text's verbal sense to the theological reality that confronted historical Israel in evoking this witness. In a word, the true literal sense of an Old Testament text is far removed from a flat, rationalistic historical reconstruction, as is so often suggested under the guise of a literal reading.

Secondly, there is another avenue into the Christian Bible that does not in itself contradict the literal/historical reading, but rather extends it. This reading emerges from the recognition of a two-part canon, and it seeks to analyze structural similarities and dissimilarities between the witnesses of both testaments. This approach has traditionally been named typological. It is neither a phenomenological, history-of-religions comparison of two sets of writings nor merely a descriptive history of exegesis. Rather, it is an exegetical and theological enterprise that seeks to pursue a relationship of content. For example, in terms of an understanding of God, it questions what features the two testaments hold in common, respecting the mode, intention, and goal of God's manifestations. A comparison is made, but not just on a conceptual level. Instead, a theological enterprise is engaged in which neither witness is absorbed by the other, nor are their contexts fused. Once again, a theological relationship is pursued on the level of both textual witness and discrete subject matter of the two collections.

A classic example of Old Testament typological exegesis is offered in von Rad's *Genesis* commentary. In chapter 23 he compares Abraham's purchase from the Hittites of a burial plot in which to bury his wife, Sarah, who had recently died, with the Eucharist. Abraham was forced to purchase a small piece of land at an exorbitant price, the very land God had promised would be his—but a promise unfulfilled at Sarah's death. Von Rad argues that the writer of Genesis understood the purchase of the burial plot to be a sign of Abraham's faith, that Abraham saw in the small plot of land a foretaste, or pledge, of God's future fulfillment. Von Rad then draws the parallel to the New Testament's understanding of the eucharistic sacrament as a concrete foretaste (an *aparché* in Pauline language) of the divine promise of eternal life, which is experienced and anticipated in the bread and wine.

Finally, there is a third entrance to biblical exegesis. It arises from the Christian affirmation that the Church's Bible comprises a theological unity even though its form consists of two distinct parts, each with a unique voice. The pursuit of this theological relationship provides the focus for critically engaging this dimension of exegesis. A level of theological construction is brought together in reflection and the full reality of scripture's subject matter, gained from a close hearing of each separate testament, is explored. I am *not* suggesting that the reader engage in a flight of creative exploration by which to enter a world reimaged by so-called "liberating imagination." This widely acclaimed approach shares all of the assumptions and fatal weaknesses of Protestant theological liberalism and is a delusion of human *hubris.*

Rather, I am suggesting, that confronting the subject matter of the two discrete witnesses creates a necessity for the interpreter to encounter the biblical text from the full knowledge of the subject matter gained from hearing the voices of both testaments. The interpreter now proceeds in a direction that moves from the reality back to the textual witness. The central point to emphasize is that the biblical text itself exerts theological pressure on the reader, demanding that the reality undergirding the two witnesses not be held apart and left isolated and fragmented, but rather be theologically reunited.

A most obvious example of this pressure from the biblical text is found, as David Yeago demonstrated in his article "The New Testament and Nicene Dogma: A Contribution to the Recovery of Theological Exegesis" in *Pro Ecclesia* (vol. 3, Sp. '94, pp. 152–164) in the Church's formulation of a Trinitarian Doctrine of God as a response to the biblical testimony. Similarly, to speak of the Old Testament's witness to Jesus Christ is to move beyond the Hebrew prophets' testimony to a coming royal ruler. Rather, in light of the life, death, and resurrection of Jesus Christ in the history of Israel, the texts of both testaments, in their fragmentary testimony to God's mysterious purpose of a new creation, take on fresh life. Thus, when the interpreter moves from the reality of God manifested in action back to the Scriptures for further illumination of the divine plan, he or she is constrained to listen for a new song—a song that breaks forth from the same ancient sacred texts of Israel. As a consequence, in spite of generations of scholarly denial, few Christians can read Isaiah 53 without sensing its amazing morphological fit with the passion of Jesus Christ.

In this case, the interpreter is using Scripture as an authoritative collection of sacred writings that have been given a special role within the Christian community of faith as the continuing vehicle of divine manifestation. The text of Scripture, when infused by the Spirit with the full ontological reality of God, resonates with a fresh voice and evokes from its hearers the response of praise and wonder. This voice, which transcends historical origins, calls forth the hymns, liturgy, and art of the Church in ever-changing forms of grateful response. This is her source of praise and thanksgiving. Its genre is confession, not apologetics; its function is worship, not disputation; its content is eschatology, not time bound history; and its truth is self-affirming, not analytical, demonstration.

If this description of the nature of truly theological exegesis is to any degree convincing, then the conclusion is inescapable. Our modern critical understanding of the task of exegesis, whether on the left or right of the theological spectrum, needs major overhauling. To simply suggest minor adjustments is hopelessly inadequate for doing justice to the true goals of interpretation and will result only in the repetition of past failures. At a very minimum, this description implies that biblical interpretation cannot continue in its present isolation, cut off from the essential aid of Church history, patristics, dogmatics, and homiletics, but must strive to combine its discipline with the widest possible context of rigorous theological training in the service of the Church and world.

Creed, Scripture, and "Historical Jesus"

Christopher Seitz   *"in accordance with the Scriptures"*

T here are three aspects of the phrase, "in accordance with the Scriptures," found in the Nicene Creed, to which I would like to draw attention. The first is its biblical character. "In accordance with the Scriptures" is a phrase lifted bodily from 1 Corinthians 15. Any sharp separation between creed and Scripture, Bible and tradition, exegesis and theology misrepresents the situation. Popular formulations like "Scripture, reason, tradition" are confused precisely at the moment three individual authorities are posited as separate affairs.

A second aspect is the phrase's exegetical scope. Although the death and resurrection of Jesus are said by the creed to be in accordance with the Scriptures, a close reading of 1 Corinthians 15 demonstrates that much more is implied by the phrase than a singular happening to Jesus, according to Scripture. "In accordance with the Scriptures" says as much about the present life of the rise Lord and his relationship to us as it does about dramatic Easter events long ago.

And finally, the phrase has theological significance, especially in light of modern historical research on Jesus, and projects like the Jesus Seminar. To say that Jesus Christ died and rose again in accordance with Scripture means that his identity is tied up with both Old Testament statements and post-Easter convictions. These accordances, preceding and following his earthly life, neither have been nor ever can be impediments to understanding Jesus as a figure of time and space. "Historical Jesus," it is argued, is an anachronism from the late modern period, that has been retrojected artificially into the antique environment and then called "historical" after the fashion of our present intellectual concerns. "In accordance with the Scriptures" is shorthand for "in accordance with the reality for which God requires our conformity and our obedience." As Jesus was in accordance with Scripture, so the church lives in accordance with the Jesus canonically presented and shared with believers through the work of the Holy Spirit.

The creed I recited growing up, from the Episcopal *Book of Common Prayer* (1928), was worded at this juncture, "and the third day he rose again according to the Scriptures," I assumed what was meant by this was: A lot of people had different opinions about Jesus' death at the time, but *according to the New Testament* Jesus died and then rose again. In other words, a claim was being made specifically Christian by sources about the nature of Jesus' death, namely, that it was not the final word. Not, at least, "according to the Scriptures."

But that is not what the creed means, and here the newer English rendering points better to the intended sense. "In accordance with the Scriptures" means, consistent with the plain-sense claims, according not to the New Testament, but to the Old. When the New Testament was written the Old Testament was not yet sufficiently old. Therefore it was referred to generically as "the Scriptures." It is in this sense that the creed speaks of "Scriptures," that with which Jesus' death and resurrection are in accordance.

The fact that the creed does not say "and he rose again in accordance with the Old Testament" might call for comment, since the creed is late enough to presuppose a two-testament canon of Scripture, carrying the names of the two different testaments with which we are now familiar. But it doesn't, and this is significant. Here, more than at other points, we see the exegetical character of the creed. The phrase "on the third day he rose again in accordance with the Scriptures" is derived from 1 Corinthians 15:3, where Paul says: "For I handed on to you as of first importance what I had in turn received: that Christ died for our sins in accordance with the Scriptures, and that he was buried, and that he was raised on the third day in accordance with the Scriptures"

Other lines from the creed are based on the claims of Scripture, both New Testament and Old. But this one is a direct quotation from Paul's letter, and the actual content of the quotation reflects an assertion about the importance of Jesus' resurrection vis-à-vis the prior claims of Scripture. In that sense, this line from the creed is unique. It quotes from New Testament Scripture a confession grounded in Old Testament accordance.

What does "and he rose again in accordance with the Scriptures" mean? In some ways I have begun already to answer the question. By clarifying that a claim is being made about Jesus' death, I am saying that it is consistent with the prior plain-sense claims of the Old Testament. I will explore this a bit more, but first I want to comment on a prior matter.

The creed could have adopted a shorthand at this point and let the phrase out, moving directly from "on the third day he rose again" to "and ascended into heaven." The Apostles' Creed does just that. The pressure to be more explicit could have come from the community's awareness of the plain sense of Paul's statements in 1 Corinthians 15. Notice that in 1 Corinthians the phrase appears twice in close quarters—first in relationship to Jesus' death for our sins (v. 3), and then in relationship to his burial and raising (v. 4). In other words, Paul is not just salting his assertions. He wants us to know that precisely these critical episodes—death, burial, and resurrection—were in "accordance with the Scriptures." Because the Nicene Creed accepts as a given not just the memory of statements like these from Paul's, or Jesus', but also their status as Scripture from a canonical New Testament, Paul's exact phrasing was not shortchanged at this critical point, but carried over word by word.

One explanation for the phrase, in conjunction with these episodes (both in Paul and in the creed following him), is that they were the ones demanding the most careful defense as congruent with or provable by the Old Testament. Christian faith was obliged to make an assertion about Jesus' death and resurrection as in accordance with Scripture, precisely to counter the claims of faithful Jews, to whom these Scriptures were entrusted (Rom 3:2). In other words, the plain-sense claims of the Old Testament could be squared with a dying and risen Messiah only with difficulty. Along these same lines, it has been argued that one of the earliest levels of New Testament tradition consisted of a collection of Old Testament proof-texts; Their point was to prove that Jesus was indeed the promised Christ of the Scriptures of Israel.[1] The more general view of the matter understands, as von Capenhausen once put it, that the problem facing the Early Church was not what to do with the Old Testament. Rather, in the face of a scriptural legacy everywhere seen to be God's very word, it was what one was to do with Jesus?[2] In this sort of climate, the creed asserts that the stickiest moments in the life and ministry of Jesus—his death and resurrection— were fully congruent with the Old Testament and its presentation of the Christ to come. Isaiah 53:5–12 speaks of an expiatory death; Hosea 6:2 and Psalm 16:10 are likewise pressed into service as proof-texts from the Old Testament, demonstrations that Jesus' death and rising were "in accordance with the Scriptures." The annotation in modern versions of the New Testament lists these texts as standing behind Paul's claims in 1 Corinthians.

I do not want to dispute this way of understanding the character of scriptural accordance, but I believe it is exegetically too narrow and theologically too functional a view of the matter. One should note in this regard that if the case rested on just a scattering of proof-texts to establish congruence between Jesus' resurrection and the plain sense of Scripture, the case might well prove unconvincing. The problem with this way of understanding the issue is that it has picked up the wrong end of the stick. It has failed to understand what is at stake in Paul's larger argument in 1 Corinthians 15, where the phrases appear.

So what does it mean when Paul asserts that what he received of first importance was Christ's death and resurrection in accordance with the Scriptures? We have to get the sense of direction right. It was not so much that a straight line pushed forward from the Old Testament to Jesus' death and resurrection, and could compel faith on those terms. It failed to do this in the instance of Judaism, instead birthing an entire collateral faith and community, and bringing much anguish to Paul (Romans 9–11). Rather, in the light of Jesus' death and resurrection, the inherited Scriptures were seen from a different angle. They did not predict his death and resurrection in a straightforward manner, nor does the creed say they did. Jesus' death and resurrection are congruent with Scripture. The accordance is not about scattered proof-texts, but about a much broader skein of convictions, which involve God: the agency of God, the relationship of God to Jesus, and the present life of Jesus in relationship to the Father until the Second Coming. "In accordance with the Scriptures" means "related to claims about God and God's promises as presented in the Old Testament scriptures"— not individual proof-texts about the details of Jesus' death, burial, and resurrection. To speak of God's raising Jesus is to ask how such a resurrection fits into a larger scriptural depiction of God's plans with the world.

This becomes clear when one follows Paul's larger argument in 1 Corinthians 15. There we see that Christ's resurrection is *not* significant because it is a singular event, focused on one moment for him alone. To say that Christ rose again on the third day is not to make a statement about only him, as though he had been elevated to heroic status and was now worthy of homage. It should be remembered that Herod was convinced that John the Baptist had been raised form the dead and that his powers were at work in Jesus' miracles and ministry. Others were persuaded that Elijah had been raised, or would be. Lazarus was raised by Jesus in John's account. By contrast, to say that Jesus rose "in accordance with the Scriptures" stipulates how we are to understand his specific raising. That singular event was also extraordinarily social and implicative of the entire creation, at once the most singular and most unsingular event that ever occurred, without analogy to Lazarus' actual raising or Elijah's and John's theoretical one.

In verses 12–28 Paul focuses on the fact of Jesus' resurrection—not as a fact unto itself, but as a fact inextricably related to the general resurrection of those united in baptism to his death and rising. To say that Jesus' resurrection accords with Scripture, which is where Paul begins his argument, means that the Scriptures are where the answer can be found about what God is presently doing in Jesus and in those baptized into his death. Apparently there were those in the Corinthian community who were ready to say that Christ had been raised. What they did not believe was that his resurrection had anything to do with them and their life and death. But for Paul, to say that Jesus died and rose "in accordance with the Scriptures" was to forbid such an understanding. If, "according to the Scriptures," all died in Adam, then the reverse would equally be true and in accord with Scripture: that Jesus Christ was the new Adam in whom all would be made alive. Christ's rising was not an isolated harvest, but the firstfruits of a much broader harvest, to which those in him would belong. Furthermore, Jesus' death and resurrection "in accordance with the Scriptures" means that those in Christ are presently living between two times: the time of Christ as firstfruits and the final time, when those who belong to Christ will be united with him upon his coming again. That God had not brought the curtain down on time and space was not a fact out of accordance with Scripture, but was consistent with God's delayed action in bringing in the Gentiles. Jesus' death and resurrection were in accord with Scripture, in accord with God's own statements about how he intended the Christ to rule.

What actually happens during this meantime? Scripture provides the "accorded" response. The meantime is a time when God puts all things in subjection to Christ. Then, at the end Christ will hand the kingdom over to God the Father, "after he has destroyed every authority and power" (v. 24). This scenario, with its bundle of related convictions, spells out what is meant by God raising Jesus on the third day "in accordance with the Scriptures." Paul means—and the creed supports him—that Christ's death and resurrection have implications whose lineaments can be seen in Scripture. This is nowhere clearer, for example, than in the motif of God's subjecting all things to Christ—all things, that is, with the exception of God himself. Here Paul explicitly takes his bearings from Scripture: "But when it [Psalm 8:6] says 'All things are put in subjection,'" it is plain that this does not include the one who put all things in subjection under him.

In order to understand what Jesus' resurrection entails, Paul searches the Scriptures for clues. To begin his argument by asserting that Jesus died for our sins and rose "in accordance with the Scriptures" is to designate the Scriptures as the place in which the meantime scenario can be found. Paul then explains the final significance of Christ's raising:

> When all things are subjected to him, then the Son himself will also be subjected to the one who put all things in subjection under him, so that God may be all in all.

To say that Christ rose again in accordance with the Scriptures" is at its heart a statement about God's long-range plans, with Christ on our behalf, as this has been set forth in Scripture. It is not that a straight line moves from the Old Testament to Christ in some mechanical fashion. Rather, we comprehend what God is doing in Christ right now and through eternity by returning to the Old Testament and seeking to find within its manifold testimony an accordance with what we are coming to know about God in Christ. Once again we face the reality that the Old Testament, as Christian Scripture, is not just before Jesus, but is after him as well. It is both B.C. and A.D. because Jesus lives in relationship to the Father, to Israel, and to the world; and the Father has set forth his broader plans for the world in his word to Israel, plans do which at the center Christ stands. For an understanding of Christ's present rule and relationship to God, from the moment of God's raising him to that final point when God is all in all, it is necessary to search a first testament to learn about last things.

In light of this necessity, the problem with the Jesus Seminar is twofold. It resists the force of the Scriptures, as Paul and the creed read them, on our understanding of Jesus. And consequently, it does not take seriously Jesus' relationship to God as imprinted by Scripture's prior word and guided by that word's according potential. In order to understand he who came to do the Father's will, we should assume he took significant bearings from the Scriptures of Israel, in exactly the public form we can now read them. To ignore this dimension for the sake of massive historical sifting and reconstruction is to make a category mistake of the first order.

Here the Jesus Seminar is not a benighted peculiarity, but the logical outcome of years of preoccupation with questions of origins and evidences behind the text to that which is truly revelatory. One has every right to observe the root system of a tree. To do so, however, involves uprooting the tree itself. If, furthermore, one begins to insist that the tree is not as it should be, given the underground investigation—that the mature growth is a misunderstanding in need of correction by experts; or more enticingly, that the underground tree is the tree itself, the "historical tree"—then we are beginning to approach the logic of the Jesus Seminar, and the intellectual thrall it has exercised on culture. Note carefully that once this concern for origins and evidence is validated, it can preoccupy the right wing of Christianity as being theologically necessary in the same way it occupies the Left as historically necessary.

We should, however, stop and consider the hold the "historical Jesus" presently has on culture. Why the thrall of Borg, Crossan, and other uncoverers of the "historical Jesus"? Why? Because if "Jesus" is something to be uncovered, then the necessary conditions that require Jesus to be a source of fascination, a devoted, even painstaking, interest, have been met. The Jesus Seminar is nothing if not hard work, by any standard of measurement, even if it is shown to be toil in an unproductive vineyard. The attribute of Jesus as requiring unveiling and discovery is not wrong, but it has been translated and domesticated by the Jesus Seminar and much historical-critical endeavor. It is not that Jesus is hidden behind the words about him; however, they must be sifted and probed for one to get at the historical Jesus. The words that tell about him simultaneously convey their inadequacy, in formal terms, because of the subject matter they are trying to reach. The very fourfoldedness of the gospel record testifies to the difficulty of presenting Jesus as a character of time and space—fully man, yet fully God. But this is not an inadequacy that can be remedied through historical-critical heavy lifting because it inheres with the subject matter itself, God in Christ, who exposes our inadequacy in speaking of him, and yet simultaneously remedies this through the work of his Holy Spirit in the church, allowing the frail testimony of human minds to be a lens to God's glory, a touching of the ark of the covenant.

When Jesus announces in John 14, "I will no longer talk much with you" it isn't because he has run out of things to say. What he has said is sufficient to convey the truth about him. The discussion of the Holy Spirit in John 14 makes it clear that sufficiency will be insured by God himself, through the canonical witness to Jesus and the work of the advocate, who "will teach you everything and remind you of all that I have said" (v. 26). The precedent witness of the Old Testament will have its antecedent counterpart in the construction of the New Testament witness.

To assume that the Church is responsible for any overlay from the Old Testament on a reconstructed historical Jesus (as has been the case since the dawn of historical Jesus projects) is to set up a problem of enormous proportions. For if the Church formulates its understanding of the implications of Christ's death and resurrection on the basis of their accord with Scripture, and yet no such correlation is believed to be at work in Jesus' own case, as a historical figure, then the Church's entire faith is inconsistent with the orientation of Jesus, and with those who sought to provide the record of his life for a specific posterity, the Church.

Some are prepared to accept this diagnosis and offer an alternative Jesus, the historical Jesus. The problem is not only that this historical Jesus resides somewhere behind and is not fully congruent with the witness of the New Testament, in the form we have it, but also that this Jesus stands apart from the witness of the Old Testament scriptures and their claims about what God was and is and will be doing in and through Jesus. One could argue that the entire enterprise of historical Jesus searches began when someone decided it was both possible and necessary to extract a Jesus from the welter of beliefs preceding him in Scripture and following him in the Church, in effect marooning him in time and space. Interestingly, this was done in the name of freeing Jesus from subsequent theological interpretation. Now, however, we see the most recent project demanding fresh theological interpretation to replace what was thee from the start: a new tree for a freshly replaced root system, a "historical Jesus church" for uncoverers of the historical Jesus. The thesis suggests that here we have postmodern version of premodern Gnosticism. We again see the emphasis on special truth, the hidden unveiled, the initiation into expert findings, and the "real truth" about things. A certain piety and concern for the Church's life—less critical to earlier quests—serve to complete the picture.

Though it should seem obvious, we need to remember that a historical Jesus has never been the object of the church's faith. Rather, that object has been the triune God, revealed in Old and New Testaments and presently alive in the body of Christ through the presence of the Holy Spirit. Consequently, to search for the historical Jesus apart from the witness of Israel's Scriptures is to drive a wedge between the One raised and the One doing the raising. It is this avenue that Paul shuts off, as do the creeds, when he says that Jesus rose again "in accordance with the Scriptures."

In conclusion, I would like to make the following three points. First of all, the creeds are not just churchly efforts to identify heresy and construct a series of statements to serve as a firewall against it. They are natural extensions of the earlier rule of faith, which presented a precis of core Christian belief intended to guide scriptural exposition in the Church. Consistent with that intention, the Nicene Creed seeks to summarize and comprehend the scope of scriptural authority, as inherited and passed on. That is particularly evident in this case, where the creed merely replicates what can be found in Scripture in Paul's first letter to the Corinthians.

It would therefore be wrong to draw a sharp line between Scripture and tradition, as is sometimes done. Rightly understood, the latter should flow organically from the former, as is so well modeled in the creed. Whenever one begins to talk about fresh insights, even given by the Holy Spirit, a serious question should be raised about the life of the church and its connective tissue in relationship to Scripture, the legacy of the prophets and apostles, upon which we are built. The Holy Spirit does not provide fresh insights. The Holy Spirit is not an ongoing source of revelation. Rather, the Holy Spirit equips us presently to hear God's word in accordance with what has been revealed. We are not Mormons or Swedenborgians.

Secondly, to say that Jesus died and rose again "in accordance with the Scriptures" reminds the church of its adopted status into the promises of God begun with Israel. Far from being a problematic, outdated, or downright misguided witness to God—filled with what Jack Spong calls "examples of premodern ignorance"—the Old Testament is God's shared gift to the Church, meant to guide its present life in Christ.[3] Paul and the church understood this when they declared Jesus' death and resurrection "in accordance with the Scriptures," the Old Testament. Jesus understood this when he declared he would give his life as a ransom for many. Such a death is only comprehensible against a background of Old Testament accordance.

And finally, to say that Jesus rose again "in accordance with the Scriptures" is just as much a statement about God as it is about Jesus. God did what he said he would, and he continues to stand in relationship with the risen and ascended Lord, until all things are subjected to God and the kingdom is handed over to him. Those of us once "without God in the world" have, through Christ Jesus, been brought near and grafted into plans that reach to eternity. In Christ we are given eternal life with the Living God—the God of Abraham, Moses, Isaiah, the apostles, and the faithful who have preceded us in this place. Jesus didn't arise from the tomb like the dying and rising Phoenix; God raised him from the dead. And our rising in Christ is not to some spiritual state, but to a place of fellowship with the Living God—the God of Israel; the God of all creation; the Father, Son, and Holy Spirit.

---

[1] R. Harris, *Testimonies: Part One* (Cambridge: Cambridge University, 1916) and *Testimonies: Part Two* (Cambridge: Cambridge University, 1922).

[2] Hans von Campenhausen, *The Formation of the Christian Bible* (Philadelphia: Fortress, 1972).

[3] John S. Spong, *Living in Sin?: A Bishop Rethinks Human Sexuality* (San Francisco: Harper & Roe, 1988), 146.

The Ascension of Christ and the Mission to the Gentiles

The Rev. Dr. George R. Sumner Jr. 　"*He ascended into heaven*"

There are moments, small though they be, that reveal what is at stake in a theological issue. Something we had grown used to suddenly becomes problematic. Such a moment occurred for me in graduate school, when I received the briefing paper for a consultation to be held between representatives of Episcopal seminaries and their counterparts in a Third World country. The author, a friend, helpfully rehearsed some of the region's history, as well as a brief account of the traditional worldview. He encouraged the participants to engage their fellow Anglicans in conversation. But finally he warned that we Westerners must watch that we don't stretch our respective symbol-systems too far, for we must respect the fundamental differences between our symbolic worlds. At one level one might say, "Fair enough." (I address some of my own relatives against a receding horizon of meaning.) But on another level I thought, "How deeply odd." Who of us can imagine Paul, when addressing the Roman or the Galatian Christians, worrying about stretching symbol-systems. I believe that, for all of his good intentions, my friend had allowed other questions, born of the anxieties of his own cultural moment, to distort the very power of the Spirit to render the good news intelligible. Answering what those anxieties are, describing the shape of the resulting distortion, and reclaiming the more traditional alternatives, are the tasks of this essay.

An important occasion for this book, and for the conference that preceded it, was the work of the "Jesus Seminar," to which writers committed to a more traditional interpretation wished to respond. But if this effort has been convincing, it is because we contributors have not lingered in criticizing what we see as the crassly commercial and sensationalist dimension of the Jesus Seminar, but rather have concentrated our energies on the twin tasks of plucking up and planting, of deconstructing and reconstructing. For in order to answer not just the Jesus Seminar, but, more widely, the modern denigrators of a traditional

Christology, one must first "relativize the relativizers," to use the phrase of sociologist Peter Berger. One must take his or her claims to objectivity or scientific privilege that have survived the philosophical onslaught of our time and put them in their own historical context. Other essays in this volume show how the views we contradict come from a very particular place, from modern Western intellectual elites. Secondly, one must show how, with respect to the assigned topic, he or she can move concentrically outward to a wider and truer understanding of who Jesus Christ is if he or she starts from within the circle of a fuller, rounded faith. Without this constructive attempt from the writers of the essays in this book, our sponsoring group would quickly have devolved into "Scholarly Engaged Anglican Dyspeptics."

My task in this essay is to consider Christ's ascension, and under that rubric I want to focus on the resulting lordship of Christ over the nations, the Gentiles. In dogmatic treatises the Ascension was usually handled in a more expanded way under the threefold heading of Christ as prophet, priest, and king. Jesus' ascension to the right hand of God the Father is the image of kingly reign. In Hebrews Christ ascends as a priest into the true Holy of Holies, offering eternally the sacrifice of himself once offered. That sacrifice fulfills, even as it puts to an end, not only the temple sacrifices, but also the pagan sacrifices of the Gentiles. And finally, Jesus as prophet fulfills the hope that Israel might be a light to those same Gentiles, and he summons them to the new Jerusalem of the end time. Isaiah foresees the Gentiles flowing up to Zion (2:1–5). The Psalmist tells Israel to "say among the nations 'the Lord reigns' . . . for he will judge the peoples with his truth" (96:10,13). To say that the risen Jesus Christ is ascended is to affirm his lordship over all the nations in fulfillment of such prophetic hopes. Now is the awaited time, and so now the Gentile mission is ignited. At the close of the Gospel of Matthew, the risen Lord claims "all authority in heaven and earth" and then says "go therefore and make disciples of all nations."

Thomas Torrance, in his book called *Space, Time, and Resurrection*, has several helpful observations about this mission.[1] First, he points out that the New Testament speaks of Parousia, the Coming of God's Son, only in the singular—there is only "the Coming." The coming in the incarnation, his coming back to us in the resurrection, and his final coming in glory, are, in a sense, a single event, a single event articulated with seasons. Professor Brevard Childs has taught us to listen to the Scriptures as one witness, but without homogenizing its distinct voices. So the classic Lucan account of the ascension has something to add, for it tells us that a dimension, a season, of that lordship is Jesus' handing over of the Gentile mission to the Church. The Coming is one, the kingly time is now, but Jesus exercises his lordship first of all by distancing himself to create a season for mission. Torrance also underscores the importance of the following lines from Paul's letter to the Ephesians: "In saying 'he ascended,' what does it mean but that he had also descended into the lower parts of the earth? He who descended is he who also ascended far above the heavens, that he might fill all things" (4:9–10).

Again we see the unique form of this lordship of Jesus over the nations, namely that even now he gives power to the Church, the sinful clay pot that it is, to communicate his presence. To say that Jesus is ascended is to say that he has the power to make himself accessible. He can communicate the presence of the very same one whose identity is narrated and rendered in the Gospel accounts. Ascension means, in part, that Jesus can break down every impeding wall of cultural difference or language so that "a great multitude from every nation, from all tribes and peoples and tongues [might] stand before the throne and before the Lamb" (Revelation 7:9). The Ascension means that he can turn the diverse babble of languages, a sign of human sinfulness in the Book of Genesis, into a united polyphony of praise. Christ's power over the nations consists in part in his ability to make who he is, human and divine, truly known by many so that they may exalt him as one.

It is with respect to the lordship of Christ over the nations that I will first address the travail of western theology and then offer a suggestion toward its reconstruction. I will start with one of my all-time favorite movies, the sci-fi classic *Invasion of the Body Snatchers.* The central image of the movie is this: the alien mother-pod is dying, so in order to survive it sends out its seed-pods, its spores, through the world. Something similar happened at the outset of the modern period. At just the moment when western Christianity was entering a period of doubt and scriptural eclipse, it was sending out its missionaries to the four corners of the globe. It took time, and sometimes conversion took place in spite of the messengers, but the mission was successful beyond the wildest imaginings of its original dreamers, the Francis Xaviers, William Careys, and White Fathers. Some, like the missiologist Andrew Walls, have noted this simultaneous contraction and expansion, this changing of the guard, and the theologian may take the additional step of discerning therein the providential hand of God.[2] My colleagues in this volume put contemporary dismantlers of Christology in the context of Europe's religious wars and divisions, in the context of its philosophical insistence on autonomy and so forth. I, in turn, would locate these dismantlers as inhabitants, since the early modern period, of one dispirited and contracting corner of the now truly global Church.

To state the matter another way, in many accounts of the history of theology, modernity, with self-conscious doubt and its worries about cultural and historical relativism, is itself thought to be the "great new fact." As a result, it is claimed that one can no longer directly appropriate theological discourse across the ditch modernity creates. On our forlorn side of the gap, theological endeavor begins and ends with the conundra of epistemology, the maze of questions about knowing, the obsession with method. But what if we start with the counterclaim of William Temple, who in his enthronement sermon as Archbishop of Canterbury, claimed the emergence of a truly worldwide Church as the "great new fact of our time"? He may have been thinking of the ecumenical strides of his time, but we can discern another "ecumenical," worldwide phenomenon. What if we took *that* fact, of the truly global Church, to be decisive in our reflection on the possibility of understanding who Jesus Christ is? I offer this as my main theme, that knowing who the ascended Jesus Christ is requires, among other things, paying attention to "the great new fact of our time." Properly perceived, this "new fact" will serve to shift our attention from epistemology to doxology, from modern worries about the possibility of knowing in the face of relativity to a different sort of knowing embodied by the catholicity of the Church and inseparable from its worship.

Upon further reflection, we see that the irony of liberal theology in the West deepens in relation to the emergence of a truly global Church. For Western Christians, weary with their own doubts and with themselves, have turned their longing gaze to the younger churches. Think of the immensely popular subject of what was first called "indigenization," then "inculturation", and now "contextualization." Originally "contextualization" was a largely practical and strategic topic for missionaries and missiologists, but Western theology proper has now fixed its gaze there, hoping to see new things, hoping to move past the old, authority-bound, tradition-encrusted, epistemologically worrisome pictures of Jesus Christ. But, if one reads the literature of contextualization, what is it that Western theologians, or even Third World theologians who have studied with us, seem to have learned? The following is from R.S. Sugirtharajah's introduction in the book titled *Asia Faces of Jesus.*

These essays try to refashion Jesus in Asian terms to meet the contextual needs of Asian people . . . they fiercely resist any attempts to apply well-established and timeless truths about Jesus . . . These Christological constructions demonstrate that one need not necessarily appeal to precedents and paradigms enshrined in the Gospels . . .[3]

With remarkable candor Sugirtharajah denies that the ascended Jesus has the power to convey who he is. But with such power lacking, the Asian theologian must construct for himself or herself a figure fitted to the specifications of the context itelf. One cannot imagine a description of contextualization more determined by the cultural relativism and the epistemological anxiety of modern Western theology. Under the guise of a pursuit of difference, the terms of contextualization—its insistence that all that can ever be seen is a construction from the context—insure that the viewer sees only his or her own self. It is as if we were doubling the irony so famously described by Schweitzer; the Westerner goes to the Third World for a rest, looks down a well, and when the Asian or African also looks, a European visage stares back from the depths.

It is not only in terms of relativism that we end up seeing ourselves. The book just quoted offers a variety of liberationist pictures of Jesus. My point is not that witness and change in the political realm are not called for, but that this political overdetermination of Jesus is a Western production. Even as a praxis-oriented reaction against the liberal Western epistemological worries, a definition of who Jesus is, in terms of political liberation, is still a definition whose direction and terms are set by Western modernity.

The task of determining how we impose our own terms, however, is not yet complete. For the other great movement reacting to Enlightenment critical rationalism was romanticism. And here, too, the non-Westerner, and sometimes the Third World Christian, played key roles as foils to our flawed selves. As has been pointed out by the great Dutch missiologists, Hoekendijk, some of the roots of the Western indigenization project do not stand up under close scrutiny.[4] Some of its pioneers were German missionaries whose attachment to the traditional culture in which they worked, from Tanganyika to Papua New Guinea, was of a piece with their commitment to *Blut und Erde,* and who fell all too easily under the Nazi spell. They are a sobering reminder that inculturation, detached from

Christology, flying solo as a pursuit of *Geist in Kultur,* is not always a benign matter.

The following summary of Chateaubriand's *Atala,* written at the very beginning of the nineteenth century, is another example of the romanticist attachment to the younger churches.

> It is the passionate and tragic love story of a young Indian couple wandering in the wilderness, enthralled by the beauties of nature, drawn to a revivified Christianity by its esthetic charm and consoling beneficence.[5]

On a more personal level, as a former pastor of a Native American congregation, I know how important a role American Episcopalians play as romantic foils for the Church. But, in fairness, my critical search ought to come home to Thebes as well; it ought to critique myself, for I am here seeking to contrast anxious Western Christianity with this "great new fact."

If we would appreciate the great new fact and so move from epistemology to doxology, we will not be helped by many of the theoretical discussions of inculturation. We will need a realism purged of the romantic. We will need to be clear about *what* is the new fact in those churches. It is not simply numerical growth, for powerful witnesses have come from churches small in number, for example, the untouchable Christians of India. The earlier part of this century, for example, in east Africa, is that expansion can sometimes be followed by contraction.[6] We should not think of the younger churches as exemplifying the fervor of the early Church (since revivalist fervor has been sporadic in Third World Christianity), exemplifying moral purity. The African village church knows of treasurers who run off with money and of pastors who sexually abuse the flock, perhaps rusticated by the bishop after taking a second or third wife. Faithful African Christians would be the first to remind us that sin is culture-neutral. So what then is it that comprises the heart of the "great new fact"? If we could lose for a moment our preoccupation with ourselves, if we could evade this epistemological envelope about ourselves, what would we see, in looking on the global catholicity of the Church, and most importantly, what would it tell us of Jesus Christ?

In this regard I believe that one of the truly important books in recent years on the "great new fact" has been Lamin Sanneh's *Translating the Message.*[7] It emphasizes that the Christian missionary movement was in large part a translation movement. He chronicles the diversity of languages into which the Scripture has been translated, and through which it could be understood by native peoples so they could hear, respond, and praise in their own tongues. He does not neglect the tremendous cultural renewal that resulted, but points out that it followed in the wake of the word's translation. Cultural flourishing and transformation are not the substance of inculturation, but, where the Gospel is heard, we should not be surprised at such fruit.

Following Sanneh's lead, we come to focus on the naming of Jesus as Lord, in a Pentecostal richness of worship, as the heart of the "great new fact." The prophet Malachi in hope says, "from the rising of the sun to its setting my name is great among the nations, and in every place incense is offered to my name" (1:11). Paul, at the conclusion of Romans, affirms that the work of Jesus has fulfilled the prophecy: "I will praise thee among the Gentiles, and sing to thy name" (15:9). Proclaiming, receiving, translating, and singing of the news, from Tanzania to East Timor, occasionally in secrecy and martyrdom, the Church praises the same person. Jesus Christ, bodily risen. *This*, the great new fact, is described beautifully in one of our evensong hymns:

> As o'er each continent and island the dawn rolls on another day; the voice of prayer is never silent, nor dies the strain of praise away.[8]

And so I come to the constructive task: to suggest what a doxological appreciation of the great new fact would mean and to state clearly what it would tell us about Jesus Christ. But first I need to clarify what I mean by the term doxology. One does not need to be thinking about the gathering of the nations into the Church to emphasize Christian understanding as doxology. What follows is a brief sketch of the ways in which several prominent and contemporary systematic theologians have used the word to characterize the kind of distinctively Christian knowledge granted in the theological endeavor.

Wolfhart Pannenberg, when he addressed the question of how one ought to speak about God in his unknowability, answered that our speech, in response to God's works, is an act of adoration. We surrender our words to God in his freedom and his mystery. With typically Pannenbergian, eschatological emphasis, theological discourse is to be conformed to the Christ-event, but, at the same time, it is to anticipate that which we do not yet clearly see, "the appearance of the doxa, the glory of God, at the end of all history [that is] . . . his definitive revelation."[9] For Pannenberg, to say that theology is essentially doxological is to say that it is eschatological, especially as one considers the dimension of religious language that will prove invariably mysterious or new because it refers to God. To talk of God is to look forward in wonder to how things shall be, and to know that they will be so by the promise contained in the event of Jesus Christ.

Geoffrey Wainwright employs the term *doxology* in a different way. For him the primary and privileged place where we are granted the vision of God is in the liturgy. Christian reflection shares this quality of praise with worship in Christian assembly. Worship is where the vision granted is sharpest, says Wainwright, and so theological reflection on doctrine is the pursuit of a coherent intellectual expression of that vision, both to learn from and to guard the integrity of the latter.[10]

Let us assume then that theological talk as doxology is in its essence both anticipatory and liturgical. I would point out that it is the nations who are gathered in this assembly of the end time and so this adds a dimension to doxology. One could call this the prophetic dimension of doxology, for the assembling of the nations throughout the world is in fulfillment of the hope of the Old Testament. This worldwide assembling of the Gentiles is the context in which theological reflection takes place, a context that is itself an eschatological sign enacted in history. Thus, doxology, far from being an abstract category, becomes an ongoing occurrence across time and continents, which theology has the task of tracing.

In a prophetically informed, doxological understanding, we see the Church of the nations, first, as a sign of Christ's power to reconcile and reunite. That Christians from all the nations are called into the assembly is itself a sign of the universality of Jesus' lordship. That his name is praised in all of the languages of the earth is a sign that the curse of Babel is now being reversed by the power of the Holy Spirit. Paul speaks of the Church of the nations as a sign of the fullness of Christ's power and glory at the opening of Ephesians:

> Far above all rule and authority and power and dominion, and above every name that is named, not only in this age but also in that which is to come: and He has put all things under his feet and has made him the head over all things for the Church, which is his body, the fullness of Him who fills all in all (1:21–22).

But *what* is known doxologically? It is one thing to say, as we already have, that because of who Jesus Christ is, the Church ought to be engaged in its mission among the Gentiles. It is another thing to claim the converse, namely that the globally Catholic Church tells us something about who Jesus Christ is. This latter question might prompt one to ask the following question: Do we know something more or new about Jesus Christ as a result of the witnesses of the Chagga Christ, the Batak Christ, or the Maori Christ? In the above passage from Ephesians Paul speaks of "the fullness [or plenitude] of Him who fills all in all." In what sense are these ways of knowing the Lord Jesus filling in this plentitude?[11]

Here we need to recall the specific theological understanding of the ascension of Jesus, the Lord of the nations, with which we began, lest we suffer an epistemological relapse. One form of that lordship consists, as said earlier, in this very power to make who he is, human and divine, truly known by many so that they may exalt him as one. Notice how this confounds the very terms of the question about what more or what new thing could we know about Jesus Christ. The point is that in more and more languages, and in ever new words, the *same* Jesus is known as Lord, so as to be praised. To suppose that we need to add arithmetically to our versions about Jesus, each culturally captive, is to think in a way conformed to the world, not transformed in our minds. In other words, the gospel itself sets the terms for the manner in which one thinks about newness. For the many things taking place in the churches of Jesus Christ across the world presuppose that the same Jesus owns the power to make himself known in many and new ways for the sake of praise. That this one risen Christ is the source of such creativity is the truly new thing (*kainon*), foretold by the prophet (Isaiah 48:7), that God is doing.

Thinking doxologically, we focus on the nations praising the one ascended Lord Jesus and see a sign, of Christ's power to overcome venerable and seemingly insurmountable divisions, between one and many, between old and new, between particular and universal. We are seeking a constructive understanding of Jesus the Lord of the nations that does more than simply criticize the critics of Christology. We may fairly hope that the light of such a constructive effort will be cast backward on the travail of our contemporary world, particularly on its intellectual struggles. In its light we see this travail as a shadow, a fractured form, of that knowledge of the ascended Lord Jesus in the Church of the nations. Think a moment: Our time is enamored of the intercultural, the global. In our time, many seek to critique all social forms by an analysis of power, often hidden, and to construct them anew under the banners of diversity and difference. Power and diversity—are these not the confused echoes of Jesus' lordship of the nations, of the only One who ascends in descending?

Doxological understanding has its seed in the liturgical and its flower in the prophetic-historical. It is, in both respects, an understanding preceded locally and globally by the act of the Christian assembly. So theology in the doxological mode presupposes distinctive Christian practices and is, in turn, constrained by them. It follows that, in the process of describing a doxological understanding of who Jesus Christ is, one must include some account of these practices. The first is simply communication and hospitality among the vast variety of Gentile assemblies gathered around the name of Jesus. Here one can only applaud efforts in our tradition, however intermittent, to strengthen this network's cords of "mutual responsibility and interdependence in the Body of Christ"[12]—the crazy quilt we all know at the local level of companion dioceses, supported missionaries, and so forth. But in this time of doctrinal crisis and rending in our communion, we may also wonder what the implications are of making this doxological network truly primary in theological reflection.[13]

A doxological understanding would not end the theological discussions of contextualization that are so popular among evangelicals and catholics alike. But it would provide this literature with a plumb line and a warning, for such reflection itself is properly a commentary on distinctive Christian liturgical practices, and therefore valuable to the extent that it enhances those doxological events. To praise the name of the Lord Jesus among the nations, the Scripture must be translated. To praise the name of Jesus among the nations, appropriate offerings of prayers, of the fruits of the earth, and of the fruits of culture in art and song must be made. To praise the name of the Lord Jesus among the nations, the meaning of turning at the font from the world to Christ must be spelled out. In the case of both word and sacrament, who Jesus Christ is for the Gentile finds its limit and norm, as Professor Childs has eloquently reminded us, in the canon of Old and New Testament, in such a way that the diversity of praise is enabled and not stifled. But contexualization unmoored, which in some general sense quickly becomes a discernment of Spirit in culture, is hereby ruled out.

Space allows only one brief example. Can one then develop an African theology of Christ as the true primal ancestor over the true clan of the Church, as do Anglican theologians Mbiti, Sawyerr, Pobee, and others? Of course one can, for in certain circumstances how else could Jesus be preached as Lord, or new Christians turn to him in praise at the waters? But note well that the first ancestor is *this Jesus* rendered in Scripture; baptized Christians may benefit by the use of some old words in the context of turning to a new life. The doxological understanding constrains even as it invites such reflection.

Likewise, one may certainly offer theological analyses from a liberationist perspective, for example, from the perspective of women and the working class in a developing country. One can and should detail the concrete social conditions involved. To its credit, such liberationist critiques can help overcome the romanticism to which I referred earlier. But such analyses cannot serve as a norm by which Christian doctrine is defined. Rather, these analyses should be understood as giving substance to the meaning of conversion and the baptismal charge that in the Lord Jesus there is "neither Jew nor Greek . . . neither slave nor free . . . neither male nor female" (Galatians 3:25, RSV). Absorbing and deploying such analyses into the Scripture-shaped world is what baptized Gentiles do.

Let us return at this point to the central theme of this volume: "the Christ of canon and creed." We have argued that the diversely contextual Christ, far from being a solution to the critics' anxieties with the "historical Jesus," is in fact a form of the same problem. We have also argued that, far from offering a truly Pentecostal diversity of truths about this Christ, contextualization offers only varied shapes to the same Western epistemological trap. By contrast, the polyphonous voice of Scripture is heard only if one first recalls the common features of all the places and occasions of those Scriptures: the unique person of Jesus Christ as the interpretive key and goal, and the celebration of font and table in his presence, as Gentile believers gather in fulfillment of those very Scriptures. In other words, we Gentiles understand the Scriptures only as we ourselves are prophetically understood by them. Within this grid of identity, tradition, text, and practice, explications particular to the circumstances of congregations and peoples can assume distinctive contours.

At this point one can imagine several objections. One might in fairness ask about the proliferation of Christian communities in the Third World. Can one really think of this development as a single, polyphonous chorus of praise? Are there not eucharistic, and hence covertly catholic, assumptions behind this vision that are belied by the evangelical and Pentecostal nature of these new churches? I would respond that the vision I have laid out assumes a bare minimum of uniformity: a common Scripture translated and an assembly in which the name of Jesus is praised. Still, we may in classically Catholic fashion think of the Catholic tradition as the fullness of communion in which all assemblies of the Gentiles share to some degree.

In a self-absorbed and forgetful time, constructive theology will always comprise retrieval, remembering. The epistemological anxiety of our time and place has the quality of a disembodied haze; in contrast, doxological understanding makes the concreteness and specificity of an embodied knowledge possible. In the second half of the first Christian millenium, the mystical body (*corpus mysticum*) was an important category in Christian thought. I believe it is closely analogous to our present argument about doxology. Whose is this mystical body? It is one body, first of all the body of Jesus Christ in heaven and then the body of the Church, whose head is Christ. But as the scholar Henri de Lubac would remind us, the term was used especially for the Eucharist, the third aspect of the one body, as a kind of mediating reality between Christ and the Church.[14] In the Eucharist, Christ lovingly rules his Church as he conforms it to his own crucified and risen self. Could we not think, analogously and doxologically, of the ascended Lord Jesus Christ in a similar way? There is on the one hand the bodily reality of Jesus in heaven, and there is on the other the bodily reality, a sinful and broken image, of the assemblies of the nations called by Jesus to praise his name and to be filled with by the Holy Spirit. Only as the cloud disperses around us can we see this very bodily reality throughout the whole earth. That body of the nations, called the Church, is continually informed and transformed to the bodily risen Lord Jesus Christ by the preaching of the word, the pouring of waters, and the offering of bread and wine. May a glorious profusion of tongues, of tribes gathered and mixed, and of cultural images borrowed and reflected upon serve to praise his ascendant name until he, the Lord, is clearly all in all.

---

[1]Thomas Torrance, *Space, Time, and Resurrection* (Grand Rapids: Eerdmans, 1977), chapter 1.

[2]See in particular "Culture and Coherence in Christian History," in Andrew F. Walls, *The Missionary Movement in Christian History: Studies in the Transmission of Faith* (Maryknoll, NY: Orbis Books, 1996).

[3]R.S. Sugirtharajah, *Asia Faces of Jesus* (Maryknoll, NY: Orbis Books, 1993), ix.

[4]Johannes Hoekendijk, *Kirche und Volk in der deutschen Missionswissenschaft* (Munich: Christian. Kaiser, 1967).

[5]This quotation is from the jacket summary of the translation by Irving Putter, Atala (Berkeley: University of California, 1952).

[6]On this see Roland Oliver's *The Missionary Factor in East Africa,* (London: Longman, 1952).

[7](Maryknoll, NY: Orbis Books, 1989).

[8]The hymn, by John Ellerton, is #24 in *The Hymnal 1982,* (New York: The Church Pension Fund, 1985).

[9]Wolfhart Pannenberg, *Basic Issues in Theology* (Philadelphia: Westminister, 1970), Volume I, p. 237.

[10]See *Doxology: The Praise of God in Worship, Doctrine and Life: A Systematic Theology* (New York: Oxford, 1980), 3.

[11]Such an appeal to this passage, to make the point I am discussing, may be found in Walls, *op.cit.,* xxvii.

[12]*Mutual Responsibility and Interdependence in the Body of Christ,* ed. Stephen F. Bayne Jr. (New York: Seabury Press, 1964).

[13]Anglicanism in the modern era has emphasized the autonomy of its autocephalous national churches, by analogy with the Church of England, but also with a self-conscious concern to protect itself against coercion or excessive control by the missionary parent churches. In a time when the the largest Anglican churches are Nigerian and Ugandan, and arguably the most conflicted and troubled among American and English Churches, these concerns seem dated. Would a doxological understanding be better promoted in a global, eucharistic communion like our own, in a time when the centrifugal pressures of modernity are intense, by a turn toward a more conciliar mode of polity? This is, of course, a topic requiring a lecture of its own.

[14]Henri de Lubac, *Corpus Mysticum: l'eucharistic et l'Eglise au Moyen age. Etude historique* (Paris: Aubier, 1949), I. L'evolution du sens de 'corpus mysticum.'

He Shall Come Again in Glory

The Reverend Dr. Kendall S. Harmon   *"He will come again"*

Eschatology is the word theologians use to describe the study of the last things. It is often associated in people's minds with subjects such as the Second Coming of Christ, death, judgment, heaven, hell, and so forth. More fully understood, however, eschatology concerns itself with the claim that in Jesus Christ and the outpouring of the Spirit, the "last days" of which Scripture speaks have begun in history. The purpose of this essay is to make a proposal for the recovery of a Christ-centered eschatology.

To call for the recovery of a Christ-centered eschatology involves two goals. First, the contemporary church needs to rediscover eschatology itself, and then the Church needs to place Christ at the center of eschatology. In proposing such a recovery, I will focus on the portion of the creed that says, "He will come again in glory." Specifically, I will concentrate on the phrase speak "will come again" and the word "He." Both of these speak to the above goals and will be considered accordingly. In concluding, I will offer some suggestions regarding the practical implications of this proposal for the Church as we approach the twenty-first century.

The phrase "will come again" suggests that the work of salvation that God began in Christ has not yet reached its glorious fulfillment. Something more needs to happen. This "something more" is not a quiet and harmless addendum at the end of a theology textbook, but rather it is the heart of our faith as Christians. To be a Christian is to be eschatological and to believe that in Christ eternity has intersected with time, that heaven has begun on earth. To be a Christian means to trust that he who came is the same as he who is coming, so that the description of Christ's people in Hebrews as those "who are eagerly waiting for him" (9:28) is accurate. Karl Barth's famous statement in his commentary on the epistle to the Romans still stands: "If Christianity be not altogether thoroughgoing eschatology, there remains in it no relationship whatever with Christ" (*The Epistle to the Romans* [Oxford: Oxford University Press, 1933], 314).

Here we reach a serious problem: If eschatology is the heart of what it means to think and live as a Christian, one has precious little sense of this in the contemporary Church. Paul Badham, a leading British thinker on this subject, describes the dilemma well:

> [One of the most striking examples] of secularization in contemporary Christianity is the quiet dropping of belief in a future life. Historically, this belief was the lifeblood of dynamic Christianity. The early Christians thought of themselves as "aliens and exiles on earth" and as persons whose true citizenship was in heaven. And throughout the Christian centuries, belief in a future life was at the heart of all living faith. Now however, this faith, though rarely denied, is equally rarely affirmed. I myself acquired two degrees in Christian theology and completed all the requirements for ordination to the Anglican ministry without receiving any instruction in this doctrine, or even being exposed to sermons about it. ("Some Secular Trends in the Church of England Today," *Religion, State and Society in Modern Britain* [Lampeter: Edwin Mellen, 1989], 26)

To illustrate Professor Badham's point, ask yourself: Am I worshiping in a community in which the people have a deep sense that in Christ a new era has been inaugurated in history? Do they have an awareness that they are merely strangers and sojourners here in this world? Are they regularly acquainted with sermons, teachings, and readings that point them in this direction? If we are honest, I believe most of us would answer these in the negative.

For a second illustration, consider the sad case of Laura Fraser, an Episcopal priest in the diocese of Olympia. Ms. Fraser became involved in the New Age movement; both she and her senior warden actively participated in channeling, a practice through which one contacts those who have died in order to learn about the next world. When asked by a reporter why she became enmeshed in such activity, she said it came out of wrestling with the fact that

> most people in the church do not believe what the church teaches. They believe a little of it—sometimes—but mostly it isn't a vital belief that changes their lives. And so, I was trying to simply acknowledge the reality of that. I was acknowledging the fact that Christianity as it is presented to most people today is not feeding people's needs. (*The Weekly* [Seattle's News Magazine], August 6–12, 1986)

If you were to read more about Ms. Fraser, you would learn that she found the otherworldly, or eschatological, dimension to be missing in the mainline world. Her bishop eventually had to ask her to leave the parish, which was divided over her new "faith."

Sadly, such incidents not only hurt the church but also reverberate out into our troubled society. Carol Zaleski speaks of "our culture's withered eschatological imagination," which she feels needs to be invigorated (*Otherworld Journeys* [Oxford: Oxford University Press, 1987], 184-185). One symptom of this disease is the state of much contemporary literature. In *Odd Jobs*, John Updike laments that we are now saddled with novels in which

> everything happens as if to tourists who can't shake their jet lag....We have lost touch with the WHY of things, and what is left is fast food for the senses and the humming brain. . . . If fiction is in decline we have lost faith in the capacity of the individual to venture forth and suffer the consequences of his dreams. . . . How rare it is, these days, to encounter characters with wills, with a sense of choice. (New York: Alfred A. Knopf, 1991)

Even more dire a consequence is found in Europe, in the increasingly common practice of people choosing to be buried in anonymous graves. These are graves, without markers or names of any kind, that symbolize people's sense of worthlessness and lack of connection with God or his Kingdom. A recent article in *Christian Century* described the widespread use of this practice, which reaches fifty percent of the population in some areas, and an incredible seventy percent in Copenhagen.

In response to this contemporary confusion, I wish to plead that we "be not moved away from the hope of the gospel" (Colossians 1:23, KJV). The creed is something in which we can be confident: He will come again! Can we recover our eschatological grounding? I believe we can, and C.S. Lewis offers us a way.

First, to recover eschatology we need to be unashamedly biblical. If we immerse ourselves in "the strange new world of the Bible" we will learn afresh that it is an eschatological book from beginning to end. In the Scriptures we are told that Abraham "looked forward to the city which has foundations, whose builder and maker is God" (Hebrews 11:10). Abraham responded to God's call because he yearned for God's promise of numerous descendants and the wonderful land in which they would thrive and flourish. As Abraham was a pilgrim following God's promise, so too the people of Israel lived as sojourners, following a God who called them their future through a cloud by day and a pillar of fire by night. This promise of God's leading is fulfilled in part as God speaks in many and various ways through the prophets, but it is ultimately fulfilled "in these last days [in which God] has spoken to us by his Son" (Heb. 1:2).

What happens in Jesus Christ is the glorious break in to history of God's Kingdom as a fulfillment of his promise to be with his people. (Johannes Weiss's 1892 work, *Jesus' Proclamation of the Kingdom of God,* was correct in the degree to which it saw Jesus' life and ministry as inextricably intertwined with eschatology.) John's Gospel points out that Jesus's salvific work follows the shape of a great parabola, from the father's glory which he had before the world was made, to the incarnation, through his life and ministry, and the cross. How is it that Jesus was able to endure the horrifying pain and agony of the cross? Hebrews 12 makes clear that the glimpse of glory the Son was given at the Transfiguration served as a reminder to his ultimate destiny, and so it was "for the joy that was set before him" (Verse 2) that he went through the blackness of conscious godlessness at Calvary and through the resurrection and ascension, to his original state of glory with the Father.

Through the ministry of the Holy Spirit, the same glorious breaking in of God in Jesus Christ is provided to the Church. Such a radical thing occurs when a person repents and believes the gospel that Paul can say that if a man or a woman is in Christ, he or she is a new creation—the old has passed away, and behold, the new has come (2 Cor. 5:17). Paul can therefore describe Christians as people whose "commonwealth is in heaven," from which "we await a Savior, the Lord Jesus Christ, who will change our lowly body to be like his glorous body, by the power which enables him even to subject all things to himself" (Phil. 3:20-21). Just like our Old Testament forbears, we too are strangers and sojourners here in this world, moving through life toward God's promised future of reigning with Christ in glory. The Revelation of John describes this: "Behold, the dwelling of God is with men and women. He will dwell with them, and they shall be his people, and God himself will be with them". . . . "He will wipe away every tear from their eyes" (Rev. 21: 3,4).

Through this survey I follow Professor Childs' insistence that the Old and New Testament belong together; seen as a whole the Bible paints a breathtaking eschatological vista. It was precisely this scriptural perspective to which C.S Lewis turned again and again. When he preached at the University Church of St. Mary the Virgin in Oxford on October 22, 1939, the background was ominous. War and rumors of war were distracting the students, and yet Lewis dared to preach that

> to a Christian the true tragedy of Nero must be not that he fiddled while the city was on fire but that he fiddled on the brink of hell. You must forgive me for that crude monosyllable. I know that many wiser and better Christians than I in these days do not like to mention heaven and hell even in a pulpit. I know, too, that nearly all the references to this subject in the New Testament come from a single source. But then that source is our Lord Himself. People will tell you it is St. Paul, but that is untrue. These overwhelming doctrines are dominical. They are not really removable from the teaching of Christ or of His Church. If we do not believe them, our presence in this church is great tomfoolery. If we do, we must sometime overcome our spiritual prudery and mention them.

Later Lewis describe all those present as "creatures who [were] every moment advancing either to heaven or hell," challenging them all, even in the context of the war, "to retain" an interest "in learning under the shadow of these eternal issues."

Yet if we are to first focus on the Bible, we need secondly to use the Scriptures properly. Professor Childs has sought to remind us of the importance of sensitive interpretation, insisting on understanding the language metaphorically and appreciating different levels of meaning within it when necessary. Perhaps this is nowhere more important than in the area of eschatological passages, where an exploration of the language's "metaphorical function" means establishing a proper balance between a naive physical interpretation of the imagery on the one hand and a cavalier dismissal of it as outmoded or outdated on the other.

With all of his training as a literary critic, C.S. Lewis manages well this middle ground between the literalistic interpretation of some conservative Christians and the imaginative tone deafness characteristic of many mainline ministers. Here he is, for instance, wrestling with the imagery of hell in Matthew 25, in response to a letter he had been sent:

I would very fully agree with your view that Our Lord's teaching is directed to influencing our will rather than to satisfy our curiosity. . . . I [do not] think that it commits us to all the later pictures of the "tortures" of hell. . . . The regular emphasis is on the *finality* of rejection or exclusion—on the negative, not on any positive, aspect of damnation.

He later adds this postscript:

To picture the foolish virgins in perpetual torment is perhaps as blunderingly prosaic as to picture the wise ones as perpetually at supper! Both are prosaic, therefore fatal, extensions of the poetic image which simply seizes the moment of "Come inside" or "Go away."

C.S. Lewis, then, represents my first goal: a recovery of biblical eschatology that is done sensitively and imaginatively. This, however, is not enough; I also wish to argue that Christ must be placed at the center of our eschatology. Professor Childs has argued that the Bible is a Christian book whose subject matter is "God in the form of the Logos." Here we return to that little word, which I submit is the most important word in the creed in this section: "He will come again." May we not forget the "he"! Such a claim may seem surprising, but since we call ourselves Christians, is not Christ at the center of all we do? Alas, no.

One of my tasks in the course of pursuing doctoral research was to immerse myself in the history of Western Christian eschatology. In some instances this was a painful undertaking, but in no way more than when I learned the degree to which the circumference took over the center in this area of theology. The field was littered with treatises characterized by what Yves Congar, the distinguished Catholic theologian, called the "physics of the last things."

What does Congar mean by this? He means a focus on the last things as "things" that exist beyond history, disconnected from our present life, and in particular a focus on the participants and the nature of their so-called existence in the future world. We can take hell, the area of my own study, as an example.

On this terrible subject some scholastic and neo-scholastic theologians would focus on a model that describes a God of wrath, justice, and righteousness who condemned those on his left hand to eternal punishment. They would then ask: Where is hell to be located? What is the nature of the fire of hell and how exactly does it "affect" the participants of hell? How do the inhabitants of hell impact each other? On and on the questions would go.

In contrast to such speculative excesses, I plead for a recovery of the Christocentric eschatology of the New Testament. Such an eschatology builds upon the faith of the psalmist who says: "Whom have I in heaven, but thee? And there is nothing on earth that I desire besides thee. My flesh and my heart may fail, but God is the strength of my heart and my portion forever" (Ps. 73: 25–26). Seen from this theocentric vantage point, there really are not so many last things, but the last one—Jesus Christ. Embraced, he is heaven. So Paul can describe again and again the majesty of salvation as being "in Christ." Spurned, he is hell. So Paul can envision the prospect of hell in Romans 9 as the opposite of his experience on the Damascus road, as being "cut off from Christ" (Verse 3) and in 2 Thessalonians as the possibility of suffering "exclusion from the presence of the Lord and from the glory of his might" (Verse 1:9). Examining and challenging, Christ is judgment, as we see in his encounter with Peter at the end of John's Gospel. Origen is therefore correct to describe the judgment as the radiance of Christ's light such that "not only no righteous man, but no sinner either will be able to mistake the nature of Christ."

Thus you have my modest proposal for a recovery of eschatology and for the return of Christ to its center. Having presented this modest proposal for the recovery of eschatology centered on the return of Jesus Christ, I will now suggest two implications of this proposal for our common Christian life.

The first challenge of my proposal is to present a Christ of judgment, a Christ who calls into question the focus and priorities of our lives. I am approaching this year the tenth anniversary of my ordination and, as I do, I have been reflecting. There have not been many breakthroughs during this period, but there have been a few. One came after an intense study of the Gospels, which revealed to me that Jesus was in conflict throughout his ministry in four aspects of his relational life: his relationships with his family, the disciples, the religious leaders, and the forces of evil. Why, if Jesus was in conflict in these areas, did there not seem to be conflict between ourselves and Jesus in the contemporary Church? Had we domesticated Jesus and made him safe? Had we forgotten the fact, as one writer put it, that the gospel not only comforts the afflicted but also afflicts the comfortable?

As an example to the importance of a judging Jesus, I think of Susan Howatch. In the 1970s she was a novelist in her forties who wrote, in the words of another writer, fat, racy novels about wayward, glamorous people getting their comeuppance. So well off was she financially, materially, socially, and otherwise, that one person said, "The field was hers." Her novels were successful and her social life was glittering with people. She was constantly in demand, and her life was "on a roll," as we like to say. Her books even sold at checkout sections in American supermarkets.

All of the sudden, however, something happened to Susan and her life started to come apart. Something was wrong beneath the surface. Her marriage came unglued, and then her daughter turned thirteen. Susan's daughter shocked her mother soon thereafter by informing her that, after careful deliberation, she was going to live with her father in America. Susan was brought up totally and utterly short. Regarding her daughter's departure she said, "It made me think about everything. I felt a complete failure as a mother. Religious conversions come in all shapes and sizes and mine was not a Road to Damascus, but a cumulative effect." She goes on to say that, "It was a most alienating, destabilizing experience. All the things I thought important, like money and success, weren't important at all. God has stripped me of everything. I became a recluse. I had nothing to say to anybody."

What happened to Susan Howatch? She encountered a Christ of judgment. She was living her life, but she had not examined it. All of the sudden something happened and Jesus Christ called the entirety of her life into question. This caused her to get outside of herself and begin seeing herself as maybe God sees her. It was so powerful and so serious that she said she hardly spoke to anybody for three years.

Susan met Jesus Christ in judgment, and it was the greatest blessing in her life. She reoriented her life with a new foundation and is now an even more successful novelist. She has been reconciled with her daughter and has recently endowed a chair at Cambridge for the study of the relationship between Christianity and science. As I think about Susan Howatch, I ask: Would she have met a Christ of judgment in our parishes?

The second implication of my proposal is to call for gospel proclamation against the backdrop of the real possibility of hell. One of the children's books we have in our house is *Madeline,* the story of a girl in Paris who needs to have her appendix taken out. My favorite line in the book is this:

"In the middle of one night, Miss Clavel turned on her light, and said, 'Something is not right!'"

In our parishes, something is theologically not right: We are ministering to people who have an acute awareness that if they make wrong decisions the consequences are serious. For this reason, when they buy a car they turn to consumer reports, and when they choose a college for their children, they visit schools and pour over data. They take the choice of purchasing a home with vigor, and they have a sense that if they choose the wrong marriage partner, it could be devastating. I still remember a conference at which the speaker said, "When you marry, your future is either halved or doubled."

Why, then, is it that in the decade of evangelism these same people have little, if any, sense that their response to the call of God in Christ could have not just serious implications, but eternal ones? There is no escape from the fact that in the Gospels the claim of Christ is an ultimate decision. God so loved the world, we are told, that he gave his only begotten son, that all who believe in him should not perish. (John 3:16). Strive to enter through the narrow door, we hear (Matt. 7:14). Many are called, but few are chosen (Matt. 22:14). Not every one who says to me, "Lord, Lord," shall enter the Kingdom of heaven (Matt. 7:21). Are we a wise or a foolish virgin? (Matt. 25: 1–13) Will we be a sheep or a goat? (Matt. 25:32–33).

These questions are unavoidable if we are to really reckon with the ministry of Jesus in its biblical fullness. I mentioned earlier that there have been unhelpful reflections in the history of Christian reflection on hell; however, there have been valuable ones, too. I cite here one example of a sermon on hell that seeks to enable people to see the seriousness of missing one's final destiny.

To have lost one's parents, to have lost one's friends, to have lost one's fortune, to have lost one's health, oh, all such losses are great! But they are as nothing in comparsion with the loss of which we speak. Even if you have nothing left to choose, as when Saint Job was on a pile of dung, it does not matter if God is with you. But if you have lost God . . . you have lost everything, both in this world and the next. You are worse than a man or woman without their spouse, a person without his or her country, a baby without their parents. (Jean Delumeau, *Le Peche et la peur: La culpabilisation en Occident* [Paris: Fayard, 1983], 421).

Do our parishes reflect this kind of perspective? Are we enabling people to come into the valley of decision for or against Jesus Christ? Are we conveying the sense that the stakes are high?

Let me conclude by citing the words of Jurgen Moltmann, reminding all of us that if he is correct, this proposal is of paramount importance:

> From first to last, and not merely in epilogue, Christianity is eschatology. . . . The eschatological is not one element of Christianity, but it is the medium of Christian faith as such, the key in which everything is set, the glow that suffuses everything here in the dawn of an expected new day. For Christian faith lives from the raising of the crucified Christ, and strains after the promises of the universal future of Christ (*Theology of Hope* [London: SCM Press, 1967], E.T., 16)

Even so, come, Lord Jesus. Amen.

CONTRIBUTORS

Christopher Brown is a priest at St. John's Episcopal Church in Kingston, New York.

Brevard Childs is the Sterling Professor of Divinity at Yale University.

K. E. Greene-McCreight teaches religion at Connecticut College.

Kendall Harmon is associate rector and theologian-in-residence at St. Paul's Episcopal Church in Summerville, South Carolina.

Stephen Holmgren is professor of moral theology at Nashotah House in Nashotah, Wisconsin.

Ephraim Radner is rector of Church of the Ascension in Pueblo, Colorado.

Russell Reno is professor of ethics at Creighton University.

Christopher Seitz is professor of biblical studies at the University of St. Andrew, St. Andrew's, Scotland.

George Sumner is rector of Trinity Church in Geneva, New York.

William Witt is visiting assistant professor at Trinity College in Hartford, Connecticut.